The Allyship Challenge

How to Move Beyond Performative Allyship and Become a Genuine Accomplice

Kimberly Harden

ALLYSHIP
Publishing, LLC

Library of Congress Cataloging-in-Publication Data:

An application to register this book for cataloging has been submitted to the Library of Congress.

DEDICATION

To my parents, Bill and Gloria:

You are with me always. Thank you for teaching me how to be an advocate and accomplice for others and how to be a visionary, not a fantasizer.

CONTENTS

ACKNOWLEDGMENTS

Though they are no longer with me on Earth, I am eternally grateful for my amazing parents, who were a vital source of love, encouragement, and humor.

I extend a bouquet of thanks to Professor Randy Massengale for encouraging me to—well actually, demanding that I—write this book, and to Barbara Crook for her enthusiastic support from the start. Thank you for the conversations, the probing questions, and wise and caring guidance.

I also want to thank Ruchika Tulyshan, Dr. Victor Evans, and Dr. Rick Malleus for their unwavering support. I appreciate your follow-ups and follow-throughs. Your emails and text messages always came through when I needed a pick-me-up.

Thank you to my network of colleagues and friends who granted interviews and provided anecdotes and insights to animate these pages. Last, but far from least, thank you to the amazing team at Allyship Publishing.

THE ALLYSHIP CHALLENGE

PREFACE

Daddy was the quiet observer. He watched people, and if their actions and behaviors didn't align, he did not engage with them. He strongly believed in the proverb "Actions speak louder than words." Maya Angelou said, "I've learned that people will forget what you said, people will forget what you did, but people will never forget how you made them feel."

I agree with both sentiments, especially when it comes to social justice and workplace diversity, equity, and inclusion (DEI) efforts. Over the years, I've heard people proclaim to be allies, but their deeds did not reflect the words that came out of their mouths.

During a meeting about intersectionality and justice, a White male co-worker (I differentiate between a colleague and a co-worker) proudly proclaimed during a department meeting that he was an ally. He said, "I'm more woke than you. I read *The Root*. Michael Harriot is phenomenal. I also gave a lecture about Beyoncé's *Lemonade* album."

I was tickled by the comment. "Why?" you ask. Well,

1. I've worked with the individual for five years and had never had a conversation with him before this meeting, which was about leadership and social justice initiatives, no less.

2. His insinuating that he's more woke than I am is a classic example of White Savior complex.

3. Listening to hip-hop and partaking in and appreciating Black culture is kind of par for the course, since most of America's music, dance, and fashion culture was built on the backs of people of color.

Rather than discussing Beyoncé and Jay-Z's marital drama (I don't even know why that was newsworthy), it would have been more productive to discuss the fact that Black culture is heavily influenced by historic injustices and by social, economic, and political turmoil. As writer Hannah J. Davies noted, "For hipster white folks, blackness is still something to be consumed but not necessarily anything to engage with" (*The Guardian*, 2019, para. 6). When I presented this quote to my co-worker, the color drained from his face and he didn't speak for the rest of the meeting.

I emailed my co-worker after the committee meeting; I thanked him for his enthusiasm and commitment to social justice and provided him with a list of resources to read in addition to *The Root*. My goal was to make him more aware and to encourage self-development. He did not respond. We continued to exchange pleasantries whenever we encountered each other, but to this day, we have never had a meaningful, authentic conversation. Silence equals complicity, but so does false outrage and refusal to acknowledge or take personal responsibility for individual bias and systemic issues.

Some people do not know how to interact and engage with underrepresented or marginalized individuals, particularly Black Americans. Some feel the need to approach me in random places, at random times, such as 7 o'clock in the morning in the produce aisle at the grocery store, to announce, "I am an ally." Yes, that has happened. Why would someone approach a stranger and make that declaration? I asked the speaker that very question. Her response: "I'm a good person."

To me, that's nothing more than virtue signaling for approval. I was curious, so I asked, "An ally to whom, and what have you done to prove that you're an ally?" The person didn't answer the question; instead, she simply walked away. Ahh, good old fragility. Fortunately, she didn't run in the opposite direction when we met up again in the cereal aisle. I thanked her for being an "ally" and offered tips on how to be more action oriented.

These were just a couple of the interactions I've had that led me to create a presentation I call The Allyship Challenge™. I started giving these presentations in 2019, and they have mostly been well-received. Participants requested more information than could be presented during a 90–120-minute workshop. They wanted a book or materials to help them grow and go from ally to accomplice. I do my best to give people what they want and need, so I decided to write this book. I hope you find it useful and that it will help you develop a collectivistic mindset and encourage you to use your privilege to better the lot of humanity.

INTRODUCTION

This is not a book about racism. This is a book about privilege: how to recognize it and how to share it. How to move from awareness to action, and encourage those around you to do the same. If these are your goals, please know: I want you to succeed.

Because privilege comes in many forms, it can be compounded, permutated, and kaleidoscoped, leaving each of us with our own special brew of perspectives. Some of us are completely ignorant of our privilege. Others of us know it very well and choose to use it to our advantage. This book is not for those people.

This book is for the rest of us: the ones who have the emotional intelligence, self-awareness, and courage to know that when one of us is hindered, we all are. We agree that redressing the balance of power and opportunity is not only fair, but long overdue; that creating space for others to share their knowledge and experience elevates us all; that a wide variety of perspectives allows us to see unexpected possibilities. We have the all-important knowledge that allowing others space to reach their full potential allows *you* to reach *yours.*

If your trigger alarm is sounding, fear not. I live in the real world. This is not a problem we can solve with a high five and a hug or a TikTok duet. Nor is it a binary problem/not a problem scenario. If it were as simple as moving from being racist, misogynist, or classist to being none of those things, the world would be a much different place.

There's a lot of noise in the diversity and inclusion space. Most of it is well intentioned, though not what I would characterize as particularly constructive. Those of us who earn our living in this field often disagree, and we often compete rather than collaborate. Organizations haphazardly try to launch DEI initiatives as cheaply as possible. This approach equates to a temporary, positive-brand PR stunt rather than to substantial, sustainable change. Let's put aside the idea of winning and get to some real talk: This is not about becoming the valedictorian. It's about creating real change and advocating for fair and equal opportunities for all.

How do you achieve this? By advancing from an ally to an advocate and taking it a step further to become an accomplice. How do you become an advocate or an accomplice? I will teach you.

This is normally the part of the book where an author defines terms or explains their perspective. If I were doing academic work around privilege, I might take some time to do that. It would be important for me use this back door to tell you what school of thought I belong to or how cleverly I can critique the work of my colleagues. But I don't live solely in academia, and you probably don't either. We move in regular circles and have to make decisions based on what is actually happening rather than on what should, in an ideal world, be happening.

What I will do is mention briefly the three main terms I use in this book: ally, advocate, and accomplice. The rest of the text will make more sense if we have a shared understanding of these words. Aside from that, I will explain everything else as we go through the material. This is a practical book, and it is important to me that you be able to engage with the material directly.

Ally

In modern discussions of race, gender, and privilege, "ally" has come to mean anyone who doesn't intentionally oppress others. In the context of my Ally–Advocate–Accomplice framework, allies are very concerned about what others think of them and less worried about converting their opinions into action.

In 2021, it's socially very difficult to argue against the idea that women and people of color should be afforded the same privileges as everyone else. What's not difficult is failing to take any action to make that happen—unless someone is watching, of course. In that case, we tend to put on an Oscar-worthy performance. Hence, we get performative allyship.

What's most important to allies is that other people think they are a good person—like the person I encountered at the supermarket. Real talk: If had a dollar for every person who announced their ally status to me while I'm squeezing a zucchini, I would never have to do my own grocery shopping, cook my own food, or wash my own dishes ever again.

Advocate

The next stage in the redressing process is being an advocate. In this book, an advocate is not only someone who publicly recommends or supports racial justice, but someone who is also willing to spend some of their social capital to push back against prejudice and discrimination.

Advocates do call out biased thinking in the moment, and then they follow up with a private word to discover why the comments or behavior are happening. This resistance to "jokes" and refusal to just go with the flow may make advocates unpopular with their similarly privileged colleagues. For colleagues who are hindered, having an advocate stand in the gap means feeling seen, supported, and more able to do their best work.

There are limits, however. In some instances, advocates may feel guilty about speaking up after the fact, or they may be unwilling to pass up a promotion. They are sometimes unprepared to deal with the social penalty for the sake of what should be.

Accomplice

The word "accomplice" has gotten a bad rap because it is often equated with wrongdoing—you know, like Bonnie and Clyde. Before it became connected with the underworld, according to *Merriam-Webster*, the word meant to be "folded in with," which, if you'll permit a bit of poetic license, is the meaning I'd like to use in this book.

Let's wander into the land of animation for a brief moment: Fred and Barney, Scooby and Shaggy, SpongeBob and Patrick, Woody and Buzz, Timon and Pumba, Mike and Sully—these are all examples of accomplices.

An accomplice is someone who speaks out and stands up for a person or group, especially those who are targeted and discriminated against. An accomplice works to end oppression by going to bat for people who are stigmatized, discriminated against, or treated unfairly.

Some people claim to support the principles of diversity, equity, and inclusion. Few, however, are courageous enough to put their own jobs on the line by speaking out against prejudice and discrimination in the workplace. Being an accomplice means being willing to act with and for oppressed peoples and to accept the potential fallout for doing so.

If an individual is willing spend most of their social capital and regularly allocate financial resources, time, and opportunity to redress the privilege imbalance, then in the context of my Ally–Advocate–Accomplice framework, that person is an accomplice. In simpler terms, an accomplice is someone who is willing to put their money or reputation where their mouth is to improve society and is okay with the risks or negative publicity that may come with doing that.

Being an accomplice takes courage and, somewhat ironically, a lot of privilege. A person needs to have resources, opportunities, and social capital to spare before they give it all away on principal.

Not in that position? Don't worry. My goal for this book is to give you the tools to make the shift from ally to advocate in the context of your workplace. You'll learn how to challenge your and others' privileged thinking, become a more inclusive colleague, create a culture of belonging, and use your power (no matter how much or little you have) to enhance the lives of those around you.

A critical mass of people making a series of small but permanent shifts will result in a much larger change than two or three of you turning into race warriors.

So let's get to it. The first part of this book is all about how to move from being a smooth-talking, virtue-signaling ally to a compassionate, accountable advocate, and then to an action-taking accomplice. In other words, it's about how to transition from being a person whose goal is to make sure others know how great you are to being one who makes sure others know how great your colleagues are.

I keep saying "colleagues" because we're going to talk about this shift in the context of the workplace. As I noted earlier, I differentiate between a colleague and a co-worker. The workplace is not the only place where the shift can happen, but the workplace provides a concrete set of social dynamics and customs that most of us are familiar with. For many people, it's also one of the few places they encounter where they have an opportunity to cooperate with people who are, in some key way, different from them.

Long before I became a DEI consultant and speaker, I developed the LEAD Model as way to think about changing behavior. In this book, we'll apply it to the Ally–Advocate–Accomplice journey; but really, it can be used for any sort of fundamental behavioral change you want to bring about.

If you've ever taken a psychology class, you'll have at least vague recollections of Maslow's Hierarchy of Needs. It's the pyramid shape with physiological needs (food, shelter) on the bottom and self-fulfillment needs (self-actualization) at the top. The idea is to ascend to the top of the pyramid; but a person can't move upwards until their needs in the sections below have been met. In simpler terms, no one is their best self when they don't feel safe. The LEAD Model—Love, Enthusiasm, Awareness, and Development—works in the same way. People who don't feel safe and supported can't do the work of developing themselves, achieving their dreams, and reaching their greatest potential.

Throughout the book, we'll look at how the LEAD Model connects to the Ally–Advocate–Accomplice journey. These concepts are meant to give some shape to the ideas that follow, not to force you into some super-rigid way of thinking.

Okay. Let's get to it.

Love

Am I suggesting that a romantic relationship with a co-worker is the key to an equal opportunity office? For the record: 100% no. I'm talking about love in the *agape* sense.

In his 1992 book *The Road Less Traveled*, psychologist M. Scott Peck defined love as "the will to extend one's self for the purpose of nurturing one's own or another's growth" (p. 85). Love is an intentional activity, an action. The bumper sticker version of this idea is "Love is a verb."

Now that we've established the context, it shouldn't be too difficult to understand why love is the foundation of the LEAD Model. But in case you're still scratching your head, let me explain a bit more. For me to be vulnerable enough to tell a person that their words or behavior has caused harm is a demonstration of love. How so? —Because my vulnerability is an investment in their growth.

In her 2000 book *All About Love*, scholar bell hooks wrote, "To truly love, we must learn to mix various ingredients—care, affection, recognition, respect, commitment, and trust, as well as honest and open communication" (p. 5). By sharing the information, I am saying, "I love you and want you to be the best, kindest version of yourself." Speaking the truth and explaining how the individual harmed me, whether it was intentional or unconscious, will hopefully inspire them to course correct and do better. Maya Angelou famously told Oprah, "I did then what I knew how to do. Now that I know better, I do better."

Healthy relationships are based on interdependence and trust. Mayer, Davis, and Schoorman (1995) defined trust as

> the willingness of a party to be vulnerable to the actions of another party based on the expectation that the other will perform a particular action important to the trustor, irrespective of the ability to monitor or control the other party. (p. 712)

In a 2015 study, Downey and colleagues suggested that when employers engage in practices that promote and embrace diversity, employees get the sense that their workplace is trustworthy. Trust leads to transparency and communication. Trust, or lack thereof, influences organizational culture and a person's commitment to their leader and their organization. Without a trusting relationship, it's unlikely that individuals will gel and transition from co-workers to colleagues, and they're unlikely to go above and beyond to help create a high-performing organization.

Francis Fukuyama (1997) equated trust with social capital. It goes without saying that a team or workforce that has high levels of trust is a more engaged and committed entity. Similarly, a person cannot engage in the Ally–Advocate–Accomplice journey if they do not first build a trusting relationship with those they seek or intend to help. That is why my encounter in the grocery store was surprising and off-putting. I didn't know the stranger who spoke to me; a trusting relationship hadn't been formed. I appreciated her enthusiasm, though.

Enthusiasm

According to Patrick, Hisley, and Kempler (2000), enthusiasm is "an external catalyst for the intrinsic motivational energy that may be lying dormant" (p. 218). The forces that lie beneath enthusiasm can be biological, social, emotional, or cognitive and can be driven by internal or external forces. McGregor (1960) surmised that enthusiasm precipitates individual curiosity, interest, and motivation to accomplish work-related activities and satisfy higher-level social, and occasionally egoistic, needs.

Think about the last time you were really excited about something. And you told someone. And they said you were silly or weird. And your sparkly balloon of excitement slowly deflated. Remember that? Although genuine inquiry can lead and further trusting relationships as well as a safe and supportive work environment, if it's not handled correctly, we can use it to inadvertently deflate someone's already fragile balloon.

Those of us who believe social justice is important and are excitedly working to make things better for those who have been marginalized or historically underrepresented or underserved are often labeled "radical." Our enthusiasm is misinterpreted; some even attempt to puncture our balloons.

This is not the way forward for any workplace. Or for any type of relationship, for that matter.

Relating to the LEAD Model, we can understand enthusiasm as believing that inclusion and a culture of belonging are important, desiring change, and being willing to do the work to make it happen. Though pom-poms are not required, we are indeed social justice cheerleaders. As anyone who has turned a spoon into an airplane to encourage a child to eat knows, enthusiasm begets enthusiasm. We must be aware and mindful of not diminishing a person or their values simply because we do not understand or agree with them.

Awareness

Awareness, or affirmative introspection, is an ongoing process that involves reaching and maintaining a comfort with one's own identity while understanding and respecting another individual's values, passions, preferences, and worldview. Gardenswartz, Cherbosque, and Rowe (2008) defined affirmative introspection as "the ability to take an honest look inward with curiosity in a non-judgmental way" (p. 44). According to the authors, affirmative introspection is the critical first step in developing the ability to deal with differences. It's self-awareness that enables us to understand our reactions to others.

Awareness is a vital component of relationships. A person who is aware recognizes how their feelings affect them, other people, and their job performance. Aware (or woke) individuals value constructive criticism and feel comfortable talking about their limitations and strengths. As psychologist Daniel Goleman (2004) noted, highly aware people are "neither overly critical nor unrealistically hopeful; rather, they are honest with themselves and with others" (p. 84).

Let me caution you: When you reach a level of awareness, it can be tempting to treat your friends, family, or colleagues as subjects for some sort of anthropological study. Taking the time to really get to know your colleagues is a not a school assignment. There is no book report at the end. Awareness and curiosity are good things, but not when they come at the expense of the other person's enjoyment.

Let me give you an example.

I have dreadlocks. I prefer to call them "locs" because there's nothing dreadful about my hair. Some people have a certain level of awareness about locs, and some people are incredibly curious about my hair. In general, I'm happy to answer questions about my hair. But I will not entertain and answer questions from a total stranger who is attempting to touch me without permission as though I'm an animal at the petting zoo. Nor will I answer a question when the answer is googleable.

"But Kimberly," I hear you say, "how can I develop a relationship with someone if I just google or watch YouTube?"

It's not an either-or scenario. It's both. You find out answers to basic questions on your own, so that when the relationship has grown to the point that I feel comfortable complaining to you about how long it takes my locs to dry, you'll know what I'm talking about. That's the moment to ask questions about whether I sit under a dryer or let my hair air-dry and what kind of products I use in it.

You need to be aware that asking a total stranger to tell you about their hair and attempting to touch them without their consent is not likely to lead to a fruitful, mutually beneficial relationship. The interaction is primarily for your benefit. You must be aware and realize that lopsided relationships don't last long and that uneven contribution is one reason mistrust and resentment creep into relationships. Aware individuals understand that, if we are mindful of our thoughts, emotions, attitudes, actions, and reactions, we have the power to change society. The biggest benefit of awareness is that when we have it, we seek to resolve the negative aspects of situations and to accentuate the positive, so we can move toward a more authentic way of being with each other.

Development

The last part of the LEAD Model is the easiest. But in many ways, it's also the hardest. Development means *doing* something. Not just talking about being more inclusive, doing the reading, or going to more seminars, but actually allocating the time and emotional resources to change your own behavior.

Although development can start in tandem with awareness, the reason I've put development after awareness in the LEAD Model is that chances of success are greater when the level of awareness is higher. In his book *Emotional Intelligence*, Daniel Goleman (1995) noted that aware people have high levels of self-confidence and a firm grasp of their capabilities and that they play to their strengths and are not ashamed or embarrassed to ask for help.

What does this mean in layperson's terms?

Development is a constant, continuous process. Individuals educate themselves and encourage others to do the same. We may not always reach our goals, but we lead more fulfilling lives because we are committed and believe we are walking in our purpose to improve humanity.

Remember when you were in school and were so excited to graduate and get out into the big wide world, free from adults ruining everything? Remember also, maybe in the deepest, darkest part of yourself, how you were also a little bit scared to leave the comfort of the system you had known for the past fifteen or twenty years and become someone totally new? You learned as much as you could about your area of interest so you could be successful and not fall flat on your face once you ventured out. That's an example of development.

Even though you show love instead of prejudice, are enthusiastic about DEI and social justice, and are aware of the systemic and institutional issues, you still may find it difficult to develop. Why? Because of fear. Anxiety. Emotions. Assumptions.

All of these things will be addressed in the book. You'll get the tools you need to make sense of everything, learn how to get others on board, and see that when thousands of regular people make millions of small adjustments, things change—for the better. First, I want you to grab your mirror, clean it off, hold it up, and stare deeply into your own eyes. Vow to be completely honest with yourself. Commit to releasing the old and to embracing new pathways and the next-level mission. Let's GO!

1

"BUT I'M A GOOD PERSON!"

Many of us have a love-hate relationship with New Year's Eve. Not with the actual day, but with the first week in January. We tend to find ourselves in a reflective mood and to think about all the things that went well and the things that didn't go as planned the year before. Then we make resolutions, the same ones we've made for the last ten years of our life: to save more money, to be a better communicator, to eat better, and to exercise regularly.

We also vow to be a "good" or better person. We make this resolution, but we never stop to unpack what that really means. What does being a good person mean? How do you define it? What are the values and behaviors of a "good" person? If you're good, then who do you believe is "bad"? Are you really committed to becoming a good or better person, or are you simply committed to having others *think* you're a good person? Organizing a youth sports fundraiser is great. But did you lead the charge and donate your own personal funds, or are you on the fundraising committee and working in name only? If it's the latter, does that truly make you a good person?

Please don't misconstrue this as a personal attack. You're not the only person who has pledged to become a better person. As a matter of fact, the NPR/PBS NewsHour/Marist national survey on New Year's resolutions (2018) found that "being a better person" was the one of the top resolutions for several years. It has shown up in the top five since 2009.

So what's with this recent fascination with being good? Did the seeds sown by reading self-help books and watching Dr. Phil for the past two decades finally land in good soil? Are we experiencing an evolution of morality? Are we so secure in our basic needs (food, shelter, companionship) that we can now focus on, and devote more time to, self-actualization?

It could be all these things. The notion of being a "good person" could also be the result of anxiety. When we feel anxious, we are afraid. And when we feel afraid, we crave binary options. Right or wrong; good or bad; even vanilla or chocolate. Adding salted caramel or cookie bits to the mix makes ordering ice cream significantly more complicated. And sometimes, that causes even more angst.

Of course, it is possible to live a full, happy life eating only the same flavor of ice cream. I certainly wouldn't complain about eating only Jamoca Almond Fudge ice cream. Where the mechanism falls down is when it comes to our perception of people.

Social psychologist and New York University professor Dr. Dolly Chugh has researched the concept of a good person and how it limits our growth.

In an interview with Goop titled "The Myth of the Good Person," Dr. Chugh answered the first question, about identifying as "good," by saying:

> The danger is that we tend to define it [good] in a really narrow way. ...Either we are a good person or we are not; either we are a bigot or we are not; either we have integrity or we do not; either we are racist or we are not. What we know as social scientists is that the human mind relies on lots of shortcuts—and those shortcuts do lead to mistakes sometimes. No matter how good my intentions are, I am going to show bias. I have internalized bias from the world around me, and the ways my bias is going to show up are not going to be visible to me. I'm going to think that I'm doing fine, when in fact I'm having a negative impact on the world around me.

Let's look at a real-life example.

Like most of you, I attend a lot of meetings. Some are obligatory, and others are for networking. My favorite ones, though, are professional development days and conferences.

At a recent DEI conference, I was one of two Black people in a room of 20. The facilitator asked each of us to write down why we were doing DEI work. Without exception, every single White person in the room wrote, "Because I'm a good person."

I confess that I was not at all surprised; I routinely hear that response. It seems that DEI has shifted from its original definition, purpose, and objective to an "us vs. them" competition. It is as though being a "good" person, whatever that even means, is now the end goal. So I called this answer out. I asked my colleagues the following questions:

- What does being a good person look like?
- Who decides who's good?
- If you're good, who's bad?

As you can imagine, I didn't get a lot of answers—or lunch invitations.

Doing something because it shows you're "good" is selfish and self-centered. The action may benefit others tangentially or coincidentally, but the main reason for the action is to let others see your goodness. Virtue signaling is a one-way transaction; it's grandstanding to receive approval and to garner or maintain a positive image.

According to *Merriam-Webster*, the word "ally" comes from the Latin word *alligare*, meaning "to bind to." An ally is someone who supports those issues, people, or causes in which they have a common interest. But what happens if you don't have a common interest? How is a one-way transaction or a one-way *anything* connecting anyone? How do we know what interests we have in common when we don't speak to each other long enough or authentically enough to find out?

I think all of us know that no one is good or bad all the time. Even Jeffrey Dahmer was nice some of the time. But we don't like this idea. It makes things too slippery.

In a 2018 essay titled "The Good Guy/Bad Guy Myth" posted on Aeon, Catherine Nichols wrote:

> It's no coincidence that good guy/bad guy movies, comic books and games have large, impassioned and volatile fandoms . . . [These] narratives might not possess any moral sophistication, but they *do* promote social stability. . . . Their values *feel* like morality . . . [but] they are rooted instead in a political vision, which is why they don't help us deliberate, or think more deeply about the meanings of our actions. (para. 12)

In other words, couching our identity in good/bad terms helps us avoid anything that we find inconvenient. Nichols also noted, "The one thing the good guys teach us is that people on the other team aren't like us. In fact, they're so bad, and the stakes are so high, that we have to forgive every transgression by our own team in order to win" (para. 12).

Do you understand how counterproductive this is? Poor behavior is excused because it's for the cause. The "being a good person" cause. The campaign for letting everyone know that you're a good person. This is why allies shout people down online or approach random people of color in public spaces just to mention their ally status. As I mentioned in the introduction, White folks regularly approach me in the most random of places and, without any warning, announce that they're an ally—in the supermarket, at the park, in the office bathroom. Anywhere. Anytime. It's bewildering, but a little bit amusing. I mean, I'm happy for you and for anyone else supporting the cause, but I'm not sure why you thought I needed to know that about you right this second. Or why you would even assume that I thought about you and your alleged allyship while I'm reaching for a pack of Charmin. Also, would you mind moving a bit so I can reach the brown sugar?

Interactions like that benefit only one of the parties: the ally. They get to announce their identity, feel good about it, and then feel hurt if their conversation partner doesn't immediately validate them. Otegha Uwagba defines allyship as "divesting from the structures that oppress Black people and unfairly elevate white ones" (p. 84). Allyship isn't just about race relations; it's about supporting and caring for all of those who have been marginalized, oppressed, and harmed. It's about justice, instead of "just us."

Constantly posting articles and tagging people on LinkedIn doesn't mean you're an ally. It just means that you spend a lot of time on social media instead of spending time doing the real work of reflecting and enhancing yourself and our community. —Alexandra S.

In her 2018 book *The Person You Mean to Be: How Good People Fight Bias*, Dr. Dolly Chugh outlined four types of good people, or allies: the savior, the sympathizer, the tolerator, and the typecaster. Here is a paraphrase of her categories (pp. 150–159):

- The savior is motivated by the "warm glow" of helping others rather than by a genuine desire to help. James Andreoni (1989) noted that a warm glow is experienced when a person feels a sense of self-satisfaction from having contributed. Andreoni called the desire to get the warm glow a selfish motive. A good example of this can sometimes be seen in philanthropy and grant-making. Often philanthropic foundations award grants but set strict guidelines for how the funds should be spent. Grantees have both the experience and the creativity to positively change their communities, but some donors and grantmaking organizations are strict and closed-minded. Often, they refuse to give social entrepreneurs the latitude they need to pivot and develop a productive program.

- The sympathizer feels sorry for someone but wants to make sure they are still in view, meaning they focus on their own feelings. They make no distinction between sympathy and empathy. They gladly feel sorry for someone, yet at the same time they feel relieved that they themselves are not suffering from the same trouble. Their feelings are at the center of the situation.

- The tolerator neither acknowledges nor appreciates differences. Tolerance is being able to accept thinking or actions of others that are different from the ones you would choose. The tolerator politely puts up with others rather than truly embracing difference.

- The typecaster does not see people as individuals; instead, they lump specific groups together and interact with the group using stereotypical lenses and assumptions, such as physical appearance or perceived success.

Reflect

Describe a time when you demonstrated each of the four modes of behavior:
savior, sympathizer, tolerator, and typecaster.

Let's think about what you've read in this chapter for a minute. You think everything's fine, that you're doing all the right things, but reading this made you realize that you might actually be harming the people you share your life with. That is probably an upsetting realization. No one likes to find out they're doing something wrong. If you feel attacked or uncomfortable after reading this, that's okay. Sit with that feeling. Awareness leads to change.

In the next chapter, we'll take a closer look at performative allyship and how that can be harmful.

Some believe that anyone who is not an ally is an enemy. But that's not a very useful distinction. This book isn't for people who are actively against equal opportunity, a redress of the balance of privilege, and the idea that we all win when everyone is given a chance to realize their potential.

I want to spend my energy instead on people who realize and agree that things need to change and perhaps don't know how to get started or aren't sure what the next step is. The first step is to determine whether you're a performative ally.

2

LIGHTS, CAMERA, ACTION! PERFORMATIVE ALLYSHIP

When I was young, any time we had to venture out to what my parents considered to be a posh neighborhood (Bellevue, Washington), I had to get dressed up. Not in my Sunday best, but close to it. It was the one time I was allowed to wear my "school clothes" to a place that wasn't school. I'm sure you're wondering why, right? Well, the answer is simple. We had to put on a performance and pretend we were just as financially well off as we perceived "those folks" (as my grandmother called them) to be. We didn't want to be followed around the store or accused of anything. We had to blend in, not stand out and be otherized.

The "fake it until you make it" ideology was alive and is still doing quite well. I would venture to say that nowadays, people don't get dressed up to go to a different part of town. Some folx, however, are giving great performances— especially when it comes to being an ally.

27

Performative allyship is when a person verbalizes their support for and/or solidarity with a marginalized group. Unfortunately, the allyship isn't helpful to that group; it draws attention away from that group, or it actively harms that group. Performative allyship is also called *performative activism*, which award-winning journalist and *Philadelphia Magazine*'s Editor at Large Ernest Owens (2017) says is "about making cheap symbolic gestures and catchy remarks to center yourself instead of the issue." Performative allyship is seen in the classroom as well. In her piece published in *The Harvard Crimson* (2018), contributing opinion writer Jenna Gray called out professors out for *performative wokeness*. She said some professors were "drowning your lecture comments with a host of social justice buzzwords—try favorites like intersectionality, marginalized, discourse, subjectivity, or any -ism—without regard to whether other people understand you."

I've observed and interacted with a lot of performative allies—socially, corporately, and academically. Performative allies are happy to post a black square over their profile picture or a meme with a nonthreatening inspirational quote in an even less threatening cursive font. They brag about buying the latest Ta-Nehisi Coates book, but they never discuss what they've learned from the book. They believe fried chicken and watermelon are an integral part of the annual corporate Black History Month celebration. They don't verbally call you un-American, but they give you the side-eye when you explain why you don't celebrate Thanksgiving and proceed to explain why they love the holiday and invite you to their Friendsgiving dinner the day before or offer to deliver a "moist" turkey sandwich the day after. They sell rainbow-colored merchandise and hang flags for Pride Month, yet they oppose gender-neutral bathrooms and support anti-trans legislation.

There's nothing intrinsically wrong with these things. To you, the ally, that behavior probably feels really nice—like you are making an effort. Maybe you are, but what if what you're doing primarily benefits you? If that's the case, are you really being an effective ally?

By now, I'm sure you have the impression that I'm not a fan of performative allyship. You are right.

Why not?

People that boast about being an ally are odd to me. It's like they want to wear it like a cape and be hailed as a superhero. But they aren't saving anyone from marginalized communities. They simply save others that look or behave like them. They avoid having real discussions about race or justice because it makes them uncomfortable. They sidestep the fact that marginalized people are uncomfortable every single day of our lives. —Neeta R.

Because it's exhausting to watch people repeatedly fail to take even the smallest action to make space for others. This isn't about intentions; it's about impact. I have no doubt that most allies genuinely want to help create an equitable, inclusive society. Performative allyship prevents this from happening.

Characteristics of a Performative Ally

Let's have a look at some of the key characteristic of a performative ally. Perhaps you will recognize yourself here. It may be upsetting, and you might get angry. You might throw the book down and say that I'm unreasonable. You are free to do so; just skip the part where you send me an email with that information, okay? Just know that anger is a cover for avoidance, which is classic performative ally behavior.

Virtue-Signaling Champions

This is essentially the "good person" myth we discussed in the last chapter. What good is doing a positive thing if no one knows you did it? What if others think you're a terrible racist because you didn't post a blackout circle as your profile? Virtue signaling is what leads people to accost disadvantaged people and announce their ally status. Genuine allies do not make grandiose announcements. They understand that actions speak louder than words. In the words of motivational speaker Eric Thomas, true allies "don't talk about it; [they] be about it."

Those who know me know I like to channel Oprah and Gayle King and ask questions. When someone tells me they are an ally, I usually ask the following questions:

1. Why do you say that?
2. Who told you that?
3. You're an ally to whom?
4. What have you done as an ally?

Brand Protectors

The Black Lives Matter movement was a massive litmus test for corporate America. Some companies, like Ben & Jerry's, Nordstrom, and The Lego Group, made strong, clear statements about their support of racial justice. Many companies have a clear disconnect between their public external statements and their internal organizational commitment.

Most organizational leaders took a middle-road approach: They released stale statements devoid of any commitment to further action. These leaders chose not to invest time in self-reflection, opted not to conduct listening sessions with employees to learn how they could help alleviate some of the trauma, or refused to review internal policies that inadvertently caused harm to Black employees. Dozens of businesses vowed to increase Black representation in managerial roles and on their boards. Few, however, have explicitly stated that discrimination and racism are problems in their company and that they will work to improve the daily experience of Black employees. As my friend Civil Rights activist and poet Darryl Moss said, "A system that seeks to destroy us can't be relied on to protect us."

Performative allies aren't concerned only with corporate branding, but with personal branding as well. Celebrities and influences have also released bland, impersonal statements about social justice. For example, one celebrity tweeted her support for Black Lives Matter. However, she was swiftly called out by a former castmate for being a performative ally. This was not the first time the celebrity had been accused of treating her colleagues of color poorly. I would say that it's time for the celebrity to do some mirror work (i.e. self-reflection) instead of virtue-signaling.

Bob and Weave

When you read "Bob and Weave," you probably assumed I was referring to a boxing match. I'm not. I'm referring to the avoidance strategies performative allies engage in. They use evasive tactics (i.e. avoidance strategies), just like professional fighters bob and weave. White fragility is essentially avoidance. Declining to change your speech or behavior because it's hard, you feel guilty, or you feel helpless is avoidance. Blaming the uncomfortable feeling you have on external sources—people, ideas, situations, location—is avoidance. Wanting everything to stay the way it was—it wasn't really that bad, was it?—is avoidance.

Why all this avoiding?

Two words: cognitive dissonance.

The psychological discomfort a person experiences when they realize that their ideal self and their actual self are not the same can be too much to bear. The frustration that allies express sometimes about "not ever being able to get it right" or "being afraid of being shamed for an honest mistake" is fragility.

Allies have the L(ove) and E(nthusiasm) components of the LEAD Model, but performative allies struggle with the A(wareness) and D(evelopment) piece. A person cannot embrace awareness and development if that individual routinely employs avoidance strategies or antagonistic behavior, such as gaslighting, to prove they are right and everyone else is wrong.

I once had a very popular "ally" tell me she was an effective leader because she's credible, and although BIPOC women have experienced many things, they're not credible. Her proof of being an ally is that she hired a Black female researcher who she occasionally allows to co-present. From where I stand, this ally is nothing more than a racist who is tokenizing a woman of color in order to win contracts, make money, and keep a positive brand image. —Patricia J.

This behavior is immensely frustrating because it is another example of privilege. Marginalized people aren't allowed to say "I'm right, you're wrong" without being penalized or punished for doing so. We don't get to engage in avoidance strategies or openly show our emotions or our frustrations without being labeled.

Chilly Climate

When performative allies communicate about privilege, they do it primarily so others will see them doing so. Though they want to be perceived as progressive on social media, they really want to remain in their in-group. Why do I say this? It's simple. As we know, actions speak louder than words. Performative allies do what the Godfather of Soul James Brown sang about: They "talk loud but say nothing."

When confronted, rather than addressing the issue head-on and taking responsibility, performative allies bark loudly and weep or wail in order to be heard and seen by onlookers. This is victim mentality. The actor (i.e. performative ally) will eventually toss the person who attempted to address the slacktivist's poor behavior into the "chilly climate." Chilly climate is social isolation that results in alienation and vilification (Hollis, 2012). In other words, performative allies tend to evade and excommunicate those who disagree with them.

The dissonance between a performative ally's internal idea of themselves and their behavior is easily noticeable by others, but usually not so much by them. Holding a mirror to this dynamic causes a lot of internal upset, which many allies react to by aggressively calling out, ghosting, or bending themselves into all sort of ideological shapes in efforts to justify their actions. This loud, shouty ally is something we see a lot on social media, where the personal consequences are low but the visibility potential is very high.

Slacktivists often choose self-righteous indignation and outrage over a meaningful exchange of differing viewpoints. They attack others they deem to be less enlightened, choosing to shout someone down or publicly shame them. For most performative allies, there is no nuance—only orthodoxy. They often deflect or deny.

So that's allies—performative ones, at least.

If, after reading the description of a performative ally, you recognize yourself, a friend, or a colleague, your role is not to shame them but to enthusiastically show love and encourage the person to self-reflect and have a growth mindset. As Dr. Phil has often emphasized, people change when they want to and not a second before. If you feel bad about yourself after someone tells you how a comment or behavior harmed them, that's your conscience telling you that you should probably make a change. This is an opportunity for you to avoid the avoiding you would naturally do and instead choose change.

If you're inclined to shift the blame and say that I'm making you feel this way, or that I'm making you do this or that, that's avoidance. Just remember: I can't make anyone feel anything, though I'm flattered that you think I have that much power. I'm not trying to force anybody to do anything. I'm just holding up the mirror.

I hope you'll continue on this journey. If you're not ready, not to worry. You've already bought this book, so the roadmap is available whenever you want to rejoin.

The next chapter is called Deep Dive. It contains a case study, discussion questions, and some questions for self-reflection. The chapter is designed to first, help you to be completely honest with yourself; second, motivate the most creative part of you to find a solution; and third, help you identify the ways you can be a true ally.

Reflect

What have you done to prove that you are a genuine ally to marginalized or minoritized people?

3

DEEP DIVE

In this chapter, you'll find a case study and several questions for self-reflection and discussion.

If you're working through this book as a group, allow members adequate time to fully read and reflect individually; then proceed with group discussion. Take the time to discuss things thoroughly and thoughtfully. You might not like what you hear initially, but giving your colleagues space to share is how we all grow.

Case Study

Liza* is a humanities professor at a small local college. She is also a member of the hiring committee. The university had an official policy of prioritizing diverse hires, so the hiring committee was very excited to interview Professor

---

* The names of some individuals and companies mentioned in this book have been changed.

Steven Cho, a promising young gender and queer theory scholar.

The interview went well, and despite being slightly bewildered by Liza's enthusiasm for mentioning that she was an ally, Steven accepted the post. Around Christmastime, Liza and a colleague bumped into Steven and another colleague in the Quad. Steven offered the usual holiday greetings, and when Liza didn't respond, he went back to his conversation and didn't give the interaction another thought.

A few weeks later, it was time for Steven's first meeting with the dean. His student evaluations were great, and his colleagues thought well of his adaptive leadership style and the culture of equity he had created in his classes.

Then the curve ball: Liza. When Steve first saw her in the room, he thought she was there as part of the hiring committee. Very quickly, he learned that she was there with a grievance.

"I'm really sad," she said. "Every time I try to start a conversation with you, you ignore me. It feels like you're only interested in speaking to men."

Steven was utterly confused. They had seen each other only once since the school year had started, and that conversation was so casual he barely remembered it. "I'm sorry you feel that way," he replied. "I'm looking forward to getting to know all my colleagues better. I have a nice pour over set up in my office. Why don't you stop by sometime and we'll chat?"

Another colleague tried to smooth things over, suggesting it was a misunderstanding. The two other people in the room said nothing.

In the following weeks, Liza and Steven did the coffee date dance. Each was on their way to something or unable to make a suggested time because of outside obligations.

At the start of spring quarter, Steven had another meeting with the dean. The meeting had just gotten underway when Liza came into the room.

Steven wasn't sure what was going on, but he could tell from the way the vibe changed in the room that it wasn't going to be good.

One of Steven's colleagues explained that there had been some complaints about Steven being hostile to colleagues.

"Hostile to whom?" he asked in surprise.

"To me," sniffled Liza. "I don't know what I've done to make you hate me. You always ignore me, but whenever you see one of your people on campus, you light up like a Christmas tree. I'm an ally."

"What do you mean 'my people'?" Steve asked. A university with a queer studies professor was the last place he'd expected to encounter homophobia.

"Why are you attacking me? I'm a good person," said Liza.

Steven was again bewildered. He looked to his colleagues for support but was met only with downcast eyes and shrugs.

After a few minutes, he stood up and said, "It's clear to me by your lack of engagement and refusal to address Liza's microaggressive comments that I made a terrible mistake in accepting this job. You will have my resignation on your desk by the end of the day."

Case Study Discussion Questions

1. Liza touted herself as an ally. What performative ally behavior or characteristics did she demonstrate?

2. Who suffered in this scenario: Steven, Liza, or their colleagues? Why?

3. What should Steven and Liza's colleagues have done as the situation was unfolding?

4. Should their colleagues have advocated for Liza, Steven, both, or neither? Why or why not?

5. What could Steven's colleagues have done to show they were true allies?

Self-Reflection

1. How often do you feel seen?

2. How often do you see others, particularly those who have an identity different from yours?

3. What is a common microaggression you have heard? At whom was the microaggression directed?

4. What's a good way to address a microaggression when it occurs?

4

MOVING FROM ALLY TO ADVOCATE

An advocate, according to *Merriam-Webster*, is "one who pleads the cause of another; one who defends or maintains a cause or proposal; one who supports or promotes the interests of a cause or group." At its core, the transition from ally to advocate is all about how to be better communicators and more empathetic people.

Because the ally-to-advocate transition is a gradual and evolving process, I designed this section to make it easy for you to dip in and out as needed. You can, of course, read it all the way through. Given the amount of internal reckoning I'm asking you to do, however, it makes sense to take it slow.

Some of you will feel really fired up and want to race through the text so you can get your Advocate Certificate before anyone else. I like your enthusiasm! But there's no certificate. Not yet, anyway. I encourage you to take your time and sit with the material. Let it percolate and penetrate your mind and spirit. Tortoises know what's what. Be like them. Processing one section fully before going on to the next is the only way to make a permanent change. Let go of the idea that personal growth is something that can be checked off a list. Then discuss your process and realizations with others. That is your trophy.

Although the process of moving from ally to advocate is not terribly complicated, reckoning with yourself can be. I don't know anyone who doesn't have complicated feelings about themselves and how their behavior affects the world around them. Cognitive dissonance is real.

Characteristics of an Advocate

We had a good discussion about The Good Person and performative allyship. I wanted you to recognize yourself in the description, if that is indeed the stage you are at, and to decide to rebel and push yourself away from that into a state that benefits both others and yourself.

There is some risk involved, particularly at the beginning. If you're not used to sharing your privilege or deliberately advantaging others, it can feel daunting. You may worry that you're doing too much. Or not enough. Once you get used to the idea of giving others a leg up, you'll soon see that in the long run, you will receive the same benefit.

Advocates are prepared to do what they can to help their underrepresented and disadvantaged colleagues, but they aren't prepared to give up everything. They have some privilege; often they are managers or career employees at a company and aren't worried about missing out on advancement opportunities. They have some leverage when it comes to deciding which colleague can access additional opportunities, but they don't usually have absolute say in what happens. Advocates can make recommendations, but they don't make the final decision themselves.

If the fight for something becomes too difficult or requires them to give up more privilege than they want to, advocates will often give up, citing external forces.

They might, for example:

- make sure colleagues get the training they need to get a promotion, but not give up the chance of a promotion themselves.

- help junior employees get their ideas heard at meetings, but only once their own ideas have been heard.

- make sure underrepresented colleagues get a chance to lead, present, and speak at external events, but only as a partner to the advocate, not as the initiator.

Allies, specifically performative ones, are so concerned with external approval for being a good person that they can't handle the cognitive dissonance that comes with getting something wrong. They double down and shift the blame. This is a massive difference between allies and advocates.

Advocates are generally less motivated by what others think of them and are happy to solicit and listen to feedback when they get something wrong. They course correct and change their behavior to eliminate the problem in future.

Dr. Dolly Chugh explained the advantages of releasing the idea of being the "Good Person" and instead settling for being "good-ish." Asked in the Goop interview why she didn't believe in identifying as a "good person," Dr. Chugh said, "I'm a proponent of letting go of the 'good person' definition that most of us have been holding on to and striving for a higher standard of what I call a 'good-ish' person. A good-ish person does make mistakes . . . but we own them and notice them when we do." Owning mistakes and doing the work to get better is the antithesis of fragility.

Advocates are aware that often they don't know what they don't know. If someone points out a harmful behavior or misremembered piece of knowledge, they listen and accept the correction gracefully. Recognizing that sometimes you are the problem isn't an exercise in self-flagellation, as slacktivists believe. When the answer is not known, advocates will take the time to find out. They listen, reflect, consider, and engage.

When was the last time you actually listened to someone you were talking with? Like really, actually, stopped everything else and listened, with no correcting, no fixing, no minimizing?

A while ago, right? Maybe even never?

Good news—it's not just you. And it's definitely not a new thing.

In a *Harvard Business Review* article published in 1957, Ralph Nichols and Leonard Stevens said, "It can be stated, with practically no qualification, that people in general do not know how to listen. They have ears that hear very well, but seldom have they acquired the necessary aural skills which would allow those ears to be used effectively for what is called *listening*" (para. 6).

So what is listening, then? Hearing happens when your brain processes soundwaves. Listening requires intention, interest, and energy. It's taking the time to recognize where another person is coming from and what they are really trying to communicate to you. The mindfulness world calls this *compassionate listening*. I like to think of it as listening to understand. As I tell my students, you don't just listen with your ears—you also listen with your eyes and your heart.

In a 2010 interview with Oprah, Buddhist monk Thich Nhat Hanh said, "You listen [to someone] with only one purpose: to help him or her to empty his [or her] heart. . . . Listening like that, you give that person a chance to suffer less." Thich Nhat Hanh is credited with introducing to the West the concept of mindfulness, a core tenet of compassionate listening.

Perhaps you feel like relieving someone's suffering is a pretty high bar for most of the conversations you have at work. You're probably right. But advocates do try. Let's dial in the context a little bit here.

Most workplace interactions are transactional. You're asking a colleague to do something related to a clearly outlined task that you've probably both done more times than you can count. Or inquiring about their weekend, knowing the answer will be roughly the same as it has been for the past 27 years. In this context, you're listening to be polite, to hear, to respond.

Your conversation partner wants information or confirmation, meaning they want to learn something or they want reassurance that they're talking to an at least semi-sentient being. Steady eye contact and probing questions about their current emotional state would probably not be welcome. But what about meetings, training sessions, lunch breaks, annual reviews, and other occasions when a deeper conversation is expected? That's where you listen to understand and can help someone suffer less.

Perhaps you don't want to say that directly to your conversation partner, but it's a good reference point to work from as you adjust your own thinking. Those of you who are considering making this quote a sign in the break room or emailing it to your marginalized colleagues, please don't. That's classic look-at me virtue-signaling performative allyship behavior. And you're moving past that.

How to listen for understanding

Dear friends, dear people, I know that you suffer. I have not understood enough of your difficulties and suffering. It's not our intention to make you suffer more. . . . So please tell us about your suffering, your difficulties. I'm eager to learn, to understand.

—Thich Nhat Hanh

Here's how to get better at listening for understanding.

First, as U.S. President Joseph R. Biden once said, "Shut up, man." We all need to speak less and listen more. Not everything is about us, nor should it be. Those stuck at the ally level disagree with this. They tend to talk and interrupt to show that they are "woke." It's annoying, frustrating, disappointing, and hurtful. Communication is a reciprocal dynamic—a two-way street. Both parties should take turns speaking and listening. However, no one said that you must divide that task evenly, 50–50. We need to say less and listen more. You can't fix a problem if you don't listen long enough and listen fully to understand the issue and the scope of the problem.

Often, especially during intense discussion, we want to interrupt and talk over the other person. An advocate knows how to be patient and WAIT. WAIT means Why Am I Talking?

Before you interject, ask yourself the following questions:

- Who in the room has not spoken?

- Is this the appropriate time for me to share?
- Is my contribution on-topic?
- Did someone make this contribution already?

Advocates amplify voices that otherwise might not be heard. Rather than hijacking an idea, they give credit to colleagues for their thoughts and offer to collaborate rather than compete with them.

Develop empathy

What might the world look like from the other person's perspective? How might that inform their behavior, motivations, and experiences? How is their experience different from how you might have experienced a similar set of events or milestones? Lack of empathy begets bias; bias begets inequity; inequity begets institutional and systemic bias.

Suspend judgment

Amazing things happen when we are able to overcome our biases, put our presumptions on the back burner, and make space for a new perspective. "During the process of compassionate listening," Thich Nhat Hanh explained to Oprah, "we can learn so much about our own perception and [the other person's] perception. Only after that can we remove wrong perception. . . . Even if he says things that are full of wrong perceptions, full of bitterness, you are still capable of continuing to listen with compassion."

We've all been in situations where someone says something that we believe is mind-numbingly stupid. That's okay. Many people don't really know what they think about something until they verbalize the idea, so speaking can be an important processing tool. And most of the time, they can hear that the idea is kind of stupid just as well as you can. And if you've never said a dumb thing out loud, then please send my regards to your fellow citizens on Planet Not-Earth. We mere mortals are very grateful for family, friends, and colleagues who let us work through our dumb ideas without being shamed.

Make space for the other person

Instead of dominating or directing the conversation, ask thoughtful, open-ended questions. Listen to the answers and do your best not to interrupt. The conversation may be about routine work things, but it may also be an opportunity for someone to discuss an unfairness they are experiencing or a struggle you didn't realize was even a thing.

Open your heart

Being vulnerable in a conversation doesn't mean spilling your life story every time you refill your coffee. That's not vulnerability—that's emotional hijacking. Opening your heart means allowing for the possibility that you might have to apologize for something or readjust your thinking. Accepting that these things are necessary and important for growth means you can trade defensiveness for care, genuine curiosity, and support.

Having a list is one thing; implementation is a completely different beast. Let's take a quick example from private life, and then we'll move on to the workplace.

Weight and body image are something I've struggled with for most of my life. My friends know this, and they know that sometimes my actual behavior doesn't match my desired behavior. When I'm having a rough day and I tell my BFF that, say, "I need a brownie right now, so help me God," she says, "Okay, great. Let's go for a walk to the bakery, split that decadent fudgy cocoa deliciousness, and talk about what's happening in your life right now." She has never said, "You don't need no damn brownie." Instead, she walks with me physically and metaphorically. My BFF knows that I need to talk and sometimes use compound cuss words without filtering myself. She lets me do that, and she doesn't judge me for it.

What usually happens is that by the time we get to the bakery, I sometimes don't want the brownie anymore because the conversation satisfied the emotional need I was trying to fill with a brownie. Notice I said *sometimes* I don't want the brownie. I have to be honest . . . sometimes I get the brownie and refuse to split the brownie. Sorry, not sorry. But the point is that brownies are great, but they won't fix the problem.

The best thing about compassionate listening is that by the time I'm done talking the situation out, I've solved my own problem.

Colleagues and peers

In the workplace, we have the added complication of power dynamics. A department leader will engage in compassionate listening much differently with a team member than with a new hire.

Although it's true that the example comes from the top, what really cements a culture change is the thousands of little changes made by regular people doing regular jobs. If you're not listening, you're not getting any new information, and without information, there is no transformation.

In a team, listening to understand translates to trust. When I know my colleague will listen to me and help me when I'm struggling, I am willing to reciprocate and help them when they need it. When we divide up the tasks based on our zones of genius instead of on what each of us is "supposed" to do, I feel seen, and I also feel that I have a chance to do my best work. As we rely on each other and are rewarded for our trust, our relationship deepens. And as the relationship deepens, the opportunities to see, hear, and hold space for our workmates increases. It doesn't feel like a waste of time or an extra task, because it's clear that rowing together makes my job easier.

It may be the case that at your workplace, everyone works in silos or there's not much scope for choosing tasks. Listening to understand has the same effect at the individual level.

Let's take the office complainer as an example. There's at least one in every workplace. All they ever do is complain; nothing is ever good enough, and it gets everyone else down. Probably the last thing you want to do is spend fifteen minutes alone with this person. But listening to understand is a worthwhile time investment, because it's what solves the problem. The complainer probably feels overlooked and unheard, and getting down on things is a way to get attention. They probably think no one likes them. They are correct. But it need not be a permanent affliction.

Too many times have I been placed in situations where leadership was not concerned with my success. They didn't advocate for me. It is troubling to think it took me over a decade to find a leader who genuinely cares about my professional evolution. It is important to zero in on your team members' strengths and advocate for them to do more—not just more work, but higher-level work, new bodies of work that will allow them to flourish. All employees deserve this, regardless of our race, age, and position. —Beatrice D.

Practicing empathy in this case means considering their position. What is it like to live in a world where nothing is quite right? How does it feel to be constantly disappointed?

They definitely notice everyone making lunch plans without them.

What happens if you just listen for a few minutes? It could be that the complainer is expressing a good point, just in a clumsy way. Maybe no one's asked them how they think the problems should be fixed. Even if nothing changes initially, at least you have some more information. And they will be a little less isolated and be suffering a little less.

Big Boss

The irony of being at the top of the company hierarchy is that you have the power to make big changes, but you don't often have time to investigate which changes would be the most meaningful to the frontline staff. People rarely tell bosses the truth, so even if you go to the trouble of sourcing information, it's difficult to rely on it. What you can do, though, is make space for your employees to talk to you. As they trust you, the reliability of the information you get from them increases, and then you can use it to inform your next big decision.

When I think of someone who really did this effectively, Elaine, a chief nursing officer I worked for, always comes to mind. Her job was to manage the nursing staff at three different hospitals and to advocate for them when management was making big decisions. There was big news to deliver regarding a change to the way nurses would do their jobs. Elaine knew that nurses would be upset and would want to vent, but even more, she knew how difficult it would be for the nurse managers in each department to deal with the fallout.

Most people would have sent an all-staff email. Instead, Elaine worked for a full 48 hours, traveling to three different hospitals and talking with every single department in person about the upcoming changes. Her fellow administrators were confused. Why would she subject herself to all that when she could have gotten the job done in ten minutes and gone home?

Elaine knew nurses; after all, she was an RN herself. She actually has a doctorate in nursing practice. Elaine knew that nurses worked 12-hour shifts (or more) and were too busy to check their email. She knew that nurses often felt like decisions were made without their input or best interests in mind. She also knew that there was a nursing shortage and that any of her staff would have no trouble finding a job elsewhere given enough of a push.

So Elaine provided the nursing staff with some face time. She was patient and answered what seemed to be the same questions multiple times. She demonstrated compassionate listening and allowed staff to share their concerns and vent their frustration. She reassured overworked nurses and provided as much information as she could. Elaine took note when several of the nurses mentioned a need and a desire for further education opportunities. As a result of the listening sessions, Elaine formed a partnership with a local university to create an RN-to-BSN program, one for which hospital staff received a discounted tuition rate. She even got the hospital to provide scholarships to give nurses a chance to upskill.

The average person (at least those of us who aren't therapists) can't spend the entire day listening to someone else's problems. However, we can and should listen more and listen compassionately. People can tell when someone is really listening to them.

How can they tell?

By our actions. That matters more than anything else.

Now is the time to talk about privilege. Not as a signal or a threat, but as a construction we all engage with, one way or another, every minute of every day.

As I've said many times in this book already, we all win when everyone has the resources and the space to reach their full potential. The trouble is, we aren't all born with, nor do we all acquire, the same set of tools. For the purposes of this book, let's define privilege as the ability to access opportunities that are not available to everyone.

Reflect

How are you advocating, not just for yourself,
but for others?

<u>Reflect on your privilege</u>

Money buys a lot of privileges. Not just stuff, but access to the best schools, resume-improving activities, reliable childcare and transportation—the list is endless. Joining wealth in the big four privileges are gender, race, and sexuality. There are of course many other types of privilege; the list is long and ever-changing. What's more interesting for our discussion of privilege in the workplace is social privilege—how likely we are to trust each other, how much grace we're extended and are expected to extend, how valued our ideas and opinions are. Things like that.

A common objection to the concept of privilege is that it demonizes people for things they can't control. Let's talk this through. It's certainly true that people don't choose to be born a specific race or ethnicity, to be part of a particular socioeconomic class, or to live in a certain environment. But we must admit that we sometimes lionize the results of that good fortune. That's the part we can change.

Another common objection in discussions of privilege is the idea that society wants to take away the privileged person's advantages. That somehow acknowledging that privilege exists means your hard work doesn't count, or that it cancels out difficulties you've overcome. Awareness is not a punishment—it's just information. What you choose to do with that information is up to you.

Allies are conscious of their privilege and are quite sensitive about it. They argue that having privilege doesn't make them a "bad" person. This is true. I'm certainly not saying that privilege, in and of itself, is a bad thing. Nor am I saying that privilege makes a person "bad." My question is: How are you using your privilege to create meaningful, sustainable societal change? Allyship should be more than virtue signaling and positive brand relations; it should extend beyond an individualistic mindset. But that's a stance some find threatening. Scholars at Stanford University found that some Whites will claim to have suffered personal hardships in order to ignore or dilute the negative implications of racial privilege (Phillips & Lowery, 2015).

Advocates choose to use their privilege to take action. The most effective advocates are reliable in their activity, meaning marginalized and underrepresented colleagues can be sure of their support. Maybe they consistently nominate someone who is usually overlooked for plum assignments, or they make sure there's space in meetings for all voices to be heard. Advocates are willing to share their piece of the pie. Why? Because they realize that their privilege routinely gives them to access to pie—and not just to pie, but also to various flavors of pie. Their colleagues, however, often have not been offered pie, or have been prevented from tasting various types of pie.

Advocates use their power to insist on terms of engagement that are fair to everyone. They realize that their privilege provides them with immunity from long-lasting consequences. There are many examples of advocates. One that stands out to me is Marilyn Monroe, who advocated for her "favorite person," jazz singer Ella Fitzgerald. When the Macambo Night Club in Los Angeles refused to book Ella Fitzgerald because of her race, Marilyn Monroe made use of her celebrity status and offered to go to the club every night if they would let Ms. Fitzgerald sing. The club owner agreed, and Ms. Monroe kept her word. She sat in the front row every night (Kettler, 2020).

Think of the fallout Marilyn Monroe could have experienced. Not only could her fans have rebelled and boycotted her for supporting Ella Fitzgerald, but movie executives could have disagreed with her decision and terminated her contract. Marilyn Monroe used her privilege to benefit Ella Fitzgerald and realized that whatever pushback she encountered would be temporary. Suspension of privileges is different from having privileges taken away. This is a small price to pay in the grand scheme of things.

"Advocate" as a noun refers to a person who *publicly* supports or recommends a specific cause or policy. This openness marks a notable difference from an ally. An ally, especially a performative ally, may approve of a cause or an initiative, but they may not publicly disclose their stance on the position, or they may avoid discussing the topic altogether because they are concerned about public relations and are afraid of damaging their brand. This applies to individuals as well as institutions.

I know this sounds crazy, but some employers don't want us to advocate or show support for our colleagues of color. I made a post on my personal social media page offering support to my African American friends and co-workers. Someone reported me to HR. HR demanded that I delete the post from my personal page because they didn't want customers or stakeholders to think the company supported BLM. There was no support or compassion. I didn't delete the post, but I did resign from the company. If they refuse to support their African American staff, I can only imagine how fast and how far they will throw me, a Queer person, under the bus if given a chance. —Dalton M.

An advocate, in contrast, is compassionate and supportive; they educate themselves and encourage others to do the same; they hold themselves and others accountable, and they engage in strategic communication. Advocates have a collectivistic mindset; allies, an individualistic one.

When I think about allies versus advocates, I think about the suffragette movement and feminists and womanists. For those of you who are unaware, Black women's fight for inclusion isn't new; we've been fighting the battle for a long, *long* time. In 1851, Ms. Sojourner Truth delivered her famous speech (or infamous, depending on how you look at it), "Ain't I A Woman," at the women's convention in Akron, Ohio. Ms. Truth's argument was that Black women were treated neither as women nor as human. In the speech, she argued that White women needed to support, fight for, and address the unique obstacles of Black women in the women's rights movement—an intersection that was (and is) often ignored.

Sixty-two years later, in 1913, the year my grandmother was born, White women showed that they still had the individualistic mindset of an ally instead of that of a collectivistic advocate. Suffragette Alice Paul planned a women's parade to overshadow Woodrow Wilson's inauguration. Allegedly, Alice Paul asked Black women from Howard University's Delta Sigma Theta sorority to participate in the event, but withdrew the invitation after she was rebuked by southern White women who would rather pull out than walk side by side with a melanated woman. Fortunately, many Black women are unbought, unbossed, and quite frankly, unbothered. Ida B. Wells, Mary Church Terrell, and Black women showed the hell up anyway.

In 1979, writer Alice Walker coined the term *Womanism* in a short story titled "Coming Apart," which was reprinted in her 1983 book *In Search of Our Mothers' Gardens*. Also reprinted in that book was a 1979 interview with her former employer, *Ms. Magazine*, in which Ms. Walker said,

> It occurred to me that perhaps white women feminists, no less than white women generally, cannot imagine black women have vaginas. Or if they can, where imagination leads them is too far to go. . . . white women feminists revealed themselves as incapable as white and black men of comprehending blackness and feminism in the same body. (p. 33)

What does this mean? It means that historically, as a collective unit, White women have not fought or advocated for Black and Brown women. Instead, many are complicit in maintaining racist and sexist structures. There are some examples of White advocates, but history has shown that most people are virtue signalers who want to appear "good" or "nice," not individuals who work to understand and overcome their personal discomfort and actively, publicly support a cause or policy that promotes equality and equity.

Fortunately, that's not all people. Let me take a minute to highlight a few advocates.

Ben Cohen and Jerry Greenfield make excellent ice cream. They also have a knack for causing non-ice cream–related trouble. Why? Because these two old hippies from Vermont have made a habit of incorporating social justice into their corporate mission for more than 40 years. The company supports a variety of causes, including LBGT equality, climate justice, democracy, and fair trade, not just racial justice.

On the "Issues We Care About" page of their website, Ben and Jerry say:

> We believe that business has a responsibility and a unique opportunity to be a powerful lever of change in the world. We can use traditional and contemporary business tools to drive systemic progressive social change by advancing the strategies of the larger movements that deal with those issues.

The company has been vocal and direct about its support of Black Lives Matter and the need for justice in the case of George Floyd. The new Justice ReMix'd and Pecan Resist flavors introduced in summer 2020 got a lot of attention, positive and negative. But Ben and Jerry were fine with that. In a June 2020 interview with *Forbes*, they said, "We respect that some people will have a set of values that are meaningful and important to them, and we may lose some customers. But what we've also learned is that those who share those values are more deeply loyal . . . actually two and a half times more loyal than just regular customers—that's of great value."

Ben and Jerry are advocates.

Actors Jesse Tyler Ferguson and Meryl Streep are also advocates. Jesse Tyler Ferguson has fought for LGBT rights for many years. In 2012, he started Tie the Knot, a collection of neckwear and fashion accessories, "as a fun way to engage every American in the fight for marriage equality" (Ferguson, 2016, para. 1). Sale proceeds are donated to support LGBTQ equality. In 2015, Meryl Streep sent a personal letter to all 535 members of Congress asking them to revive and revise the Equal Rights Amendment of 1972 to include equal rights for women (Andrew-Dyer, 2015). I don't think I've signed and sent 500 letters in my entire life. How about you?

According to a 2018 article in *Vanity Fair*, actress Jessica Chastain negotiated a pay raise for fellow actress Octavia Spencer on an upcoming film, so the two would earn the same amount. As a result, Octavia Spencer will make five times more money than she was originally scheduled to for the project.

I applaud Jessica Chastain for being an advocate. But I also find this situation incredibly demeaning. Why? Have you seen the movie *The Help*? Weren't both Jessica Chastain *and* Octavia Butler in the movie? Didn't Octavia Butler win the Academy Award for Best Supporting Actress for that movie in 2011? Why yes, yes she did. So why is an award-winner being offered five times less money??? Equal pay is a central tenet of feminism, but a 2018 report by the Institute for Women's Policy Research found that Black women earn 38% less than White men and 21% less than White women. This makes me wonder where the feminist allies are and why they aren't advocating for equal pay for *all* women.

In the *Vanity Fair* article, Octavia Spencer said, "I love [Jessica], because she's walking the walk and she's actually talking the talk." Jessica Chastain is an advocate in that she didn't compete with Octavia Butler. She believes in pay equity and negotiated that. However, there were no reports stating that she threatened to walk away from the project if Octavia did not receive an equal pay out. If she did do that, she is an accomplice, not just an advocate. Jessica Chastain said she had not been criticized by Hollywood studios or executives for demanding equal pay, which puts her in a great position to advocate for others.

Freedom from consequences is an excellent proxy for privilege.

Think about a time when you got a different punishment than your classmate or colleague even though you both did the same thing. Being late or missing a deadline is good examples. Big or small, it doesn't matter, though it's easier to compare experiences if the mistake was equally serious for everyone.

Now think about what happened to them. Were the consequences the same for each employee, or was one of them punished more severely? If the punishments varied, how were they different? Do you believe the situation was handled fairly? Why or why not?

Society has granted us all certain privileges. We decide how to engage because privilege is not a fixed state; it's situational. In-groups and out-groups, as sociologists like to call them, shift constantly. So if everyone is part of an in-group somewhere, then why do we even need to discuss privilege at all?

The answer is that there's a net benefit to being aware of how in-groups and out-groups work, and of the social conventions we have constructed around them. In-groups have the most privilege, so they make the rules. They define success, and they control the path to achieve it.

Reflecting on your privilege means admitting that you benefited from a system that disadvantages others. You were allowed more leeway when you made mistakes, made terrible decisions, or ignored rules you found inconvenient. Many of these incidents were passive, meaning you didn't actively consider that you were doing something not everyone could get away with. That, in and of itself, is a privilege. Privilege is the freedom to not have to think about what you're doing or whom it will impact. Privilege is the ability to disengage when you choose to. To not consider that others might not be able to access the same number of do-overs or opportunities to grow. On a larger scale, privilege is the freedom to never consider how the systemic denial of opportunity hurts everyone.

Otegha Uwagba, a British writer and speaker, wrote an essay in 2020 called *Whites: On Race and Other Falsehoods*. In the essay, she wrote about the Black Lives Matter movement and White people's response to it, noting:

All over the world, white people rushed to condemn, to support and affirm their commitments to racial equality. ... The obvious logic would have me gratified by these responses, satisfied that at last a critical mass of white people were up in arms about racism and acknowledging their own complicity. ... Watching so many white people grapple with the reality of racism for the very first time, I could only think of the fact that white people were grappling with the reality of racism for the very first time. ... It's galling to realise that its [racism's] main perpetrators and beneficiaries have not fully grasped its inner workings. (pp. 15-17)

Take some time to think that over. Sit with it for a minute.

The dynamic Otegha Uwagba wrote about is present in any situation where one group is in a long-established position of power over another similar group. So how do we work against this? If privilege is so deeply woven into our social fabric, does that mean it is also part of what it means to be human? Is privilege in our DNA?

Yes. But also no.

The human brain is a marvel. But it is also lazy and constantly likes to feel good. To keep from expending energy, your brain will attempt to keep things exactly the same as they have always been. This is why stereotypes and status quo biases exist. Our brains tend to actively avoid negative information. Why? Because it doesn't feel good, and if we avoid it, we don't have to fix it. This is why people often avoid doing the difficult, possibly painful thing now, even if doing it would make things better later. We have several cognitive biases—sort of default settings in our brain. These settings can be changed, and often permanently, but it takes work. Change doesn't happen by accident.

If this is the first time you're hearing this perspective, it can be a lot to take in. You may not have actively hurt others, but now you know that others are suffering. Now that you know, you might feel ashamed or guilty, and maybe also a bit vulnerable. To cover these feelings, you might resort to anger or defensiveness. This is a pretty common reaction. This is what Dr. Derald Wing Sue from Columbia University calls *emotional avoidance*.

To resolve these difficult feelings, you might feel the need to justify your behavior and make sure everyone knows by telling them that you're a "good person," not a racist, xenophobic, homophobic misogynist. This is classic ally behavior. Instead of immediately attempting to get rid of your feelings, try to sit, process your discomfort, and reflect on your privileges.

Do not fall victim to the Ostrich Effect, which refers to avoiding something because it seems too big or complex to handle or will generate too much discomfort. In the context of our discussion of privilege, this means knowing but not wanting to really know—not being honest with ourselves because we might not like what we will discover. It also means declining to take action, even after becoming aware, because the problem seems too big for one person to solve.

Instead of adopting that attitude, move toward the thing you're avoiding, not away from it. Problems are never as unsolvable as you think they are, and you are not expected to get it exactly right on the first try. Sure, privilege is a systemic problem with far-reaching effects in every corner of our society. Reading one book on diversity, equity, and inclusion isn't going to fix that. But many people listening, considering, reflecting, and engaging will.

I also caution you to not fall into the trap door of the Just World hypothesis, which is the idea that social systems are fair and that people are rewarded based on what they deserve. In the workplace, this often translates into "merit" being valued above all other factors. Is being judged solely on merit the antidote to privilege? Let's investigate the corollary: People who aren't rewarded don't deserve it because they didn't work hard or well enough. I think we all know that this isn't always true.

The question we should ask ourselves is: *Who determines merit in the first place?* People who believe social systems are fair refuse to acknowledge that privilege exists or that they have benefited from it. We need to be honest with ourselves and each other: Many U.S. systems were designed to be unfair and to maintain the status quo. The playing field has never been level. Or, to use another metaphor, we have never all started at the same starting line. If you truly believe in justice, you'll use your privilege in a selfless manner and advocate for others to get a piece of the pie.

If you want to be successful at redressing privilege in your workplace and your private life, you must decide that the work is necessary, that the pain that comes with change is worth it, and that you're committed to doing the work no matter where it takes you. Are you ready?

Be open-minded and interested

Being open-minded and curious about others means you recognize that they exist and you don't perceive their difference as a threat. This is actually much more difficult that it reads, because our natural inclination is to sort ourselves into groups. It is quite common for a person to be so embedded in their in-group that they're largely unaware that other people exist outside that group.

This phenomenon is most common in groups that have the majority of people or power—White people, for example, or men. You may perceive people outside the group as a threat to the status quo. If the group starts to look different or to reflect different experiences, then maybe whatever standing you have in this group will change. The new people might be cooler than you. Or have more power.

So far, so straightforward. Now for the complication: Our in-group/out-group scenario is extremely fluid. Over the course of a company picnic, for example, we can switch from in-group to out-group many, many times depending on who we're with and what we're discussing. Let's take a look.

The afternoon is just getting started, and as usual, the accountants are all on time. They meet up for a chat briefly at the beginning of the event, but soon, the accountants and their spouses split up into groups formed around a gender identity. Maybe at first the groups are divided into men and women, but as more people arrive, they become a group of empty nesters and young mothers. The empty nesters discover that many of them went to Michigan State University, so the group identity shifts again. Some men rejoin to talk about their university days and alumni connections.

A colleague of color stops by to say hello and mentions that they also played lacrosse at the university. Two or three more lacrosse-loving colleagues are invited over, and soon the group identity is lacrosse players. Non-lacrosse players leave the group and search out other people with more familiar life experience.

Then it's time for the intercompany softball game. All of a sudden, all these sub-identities—man, woman, mother, university alumnus, lacrosse player— are subsumed by the corporate identity. Everyone is united by their support for KLH Insurance, which, as usual, is going to crush the opposition.

As we form new groups, one of the first things we do is assign positive attributes to our identity. If we're in the lacrosse group, we might think that we're special because we like a rare sport that is so much better than something as common as basketball. People need to be special to play lacrosse, so since we play lacrosse, that makes us special.

Substitute White, male, straight, or American for lacrosse, and you'll see how easy it is for cultural stereotypes to lead to misunderstandings. Instead of excluding people who don't match your experience exactly, consider finding ways to include them. It could be that they are from a different country, or even just a different state. Maybe they have a political or religious belief that's different from yours, or a job in a department that you don't understand. Ignoring these individuals and staying inside your warm little in-group nest is easy. But it doesn't do anything to enrich anyone, you included.

Engage

Use your compassionate listening skills and find out why they think what they do or how things are done where they're from. During the course of several conversations, you will discover what life is like in their shoes. You'll understand better the oppression they feel and the ways you may have participated in it, even unwittingly. Resist the urge to minimize, justify, and deny their experience. Instead, put that energy into taking action to mitigate the harm.

Reading about diversity, anti-racism, feminism, queer theory, and so forth is great. Taking the time to read about the experiences of others and understand how they view the world is always a good thing, and I encourage everyone to do this. However, reading and engaging are not the same thing. Just reading, no matter how large the pile of books, does not replace action.

Amplify

This is exactly what it sounds like. It's that not people who have historically been underrepresented or underserved have nothing to say. It's quite the opposite, actually. But why should they speak if no one is going to listen? Often, Black and Indigenous folx, people of color (BIPOC), and other marginalized people find their ideas hijacked by someone else. A fellow DEI consultant thoughtlessly typed in a group chat that she's "popular and financially well-off because I'm not a Black woman. You have more experience and knowledge about DEI, but I have more credibility due to my skin tone." Yep, she said that . . . in a group chat . . . on LinkedIn. After some pushback, the individual claimed to be an "ally," and others interrogated her about how she is showing up and amplifying others' voices rather than just co-opting the spotlight.

Here are the actions real advocates take to amplify. They:

- recognize who in the room hasn't spoken and actively solicit their thoughts and ideas.

- determine whether their voice adds value to the conversation or if they are simply hijacking someone else's thoughts or opinions.

- ensure that their contribution is on-topic.

- openly acknowledge and give credit to colleagues for their thoughts and work.

- collaborate instead of compete.

- use the influence they have to make sure colleagues also get time with decision makers.

- mentor and coach those who have been socially and economically excluded.

Mentor

Mentorship is a wonderful way to use your privilege for good. Bringing disadvantaged people into your network and connecting them with colleagues who have similar interests and responsibilities is the first step.

Advocating for them when it comes to promotions, training opportunities, performance reviews, and so on is the next step. If you're able to, create the opportunities that don't currently exist.

For disadvantaged colleagues, mentorship—either formally in a program or through more casual knowing that someone has their back—has a powerful effect on their upward mobility.

Many years ago, I worked as a program assistant at a nonprofit international health organization. It was a wonderful place to work, and there were many people there willing to mentor me and make sure I could up my skills. I was a college dropout, but that didn't matter. My colleagues all saw my potential and nurtured it.

That is, all of them except our unit director, Ellen. Of course.

The lead director, Dr. Weinheimer, asked me to give a presentation. I said no. I was a college dropout, and I felt like I didn't have the expertise or experience to teach the material. To graduate students, no less. I mean, who was I, even?

Dr. Weinheimer did not buy my bullshit. And it is one of the best things anyone has ever done for me.

When our organization's president asked who was giving the presentation, Dr. Weinheimer said, "Kimberly is." When I mentioned again that I didn't have a diploma, she gently but firmly told me that I was smart enough to conduct the research, so I was more than qualified to talk about my process and findings.

I was a nervous wreck, but Dr. Weinheimer went with me to support my effort. I felt like I was going throw up. My mouth had never been so dry. I was sure everyone would be able to tell within two minutes that I had no place being in that room, let alone standing at the front of it.

But I started to speak. And suddenly I was in the flow. I connected with the students and had a great time. The university instructor was so impressed with my talk that he sent me an official letter of congratulations. I still have that letter. It reminds me that I can do hard things if I try.

A nice story, right? Get ready for the twist.

Ellen came back. She checked her mailbox after returning from vacation and saw a copy of the letter. She was livid. She told me in no uncertain terms that I wasn't educated enough or qualified enough and had no business representing the organization without her consent.

I was devastated. Not just because I thought I had done a good job and was starting to think that maybe I had some value after all, but because despite having worked with Ellen for five years, I had no idea she thought so little of me.

A week later, the HR director called me into the office and said that Ellen wanted me to resign. Dr. Weinheimer advocated for me, showing Ellen and HR that she was the one who had encouraged me to present. She had seen the presentation and the letter of congratulations.

I used the lump sum I received when I left to go back to college, and eventually earned my doctorate. I'm now a professor and teach senior-level research seminars.

I'm also now paid to give talks and workshops at major companies all over the country. One of those places was the School of Global Health—the same department at the same university where I gave my very first talk. It's so satisfying to come full circle, to see the fruit of all my hard work. But also to acknowledge Dr. Weinheimer, an accomplice who decried racism, defied those who wished to perpetuate it, and, by getting me started on my educator journey, helped to dismantle institutional discrimination by getting one more professor of color into the academy.

Call In/Call Out

If you've been on social media at all in the last decade or so, you definitely know what it means to call someone out. You need ALL CAPS, an infinite supply of exclamation points, and a hyper-literal reading of the thought you're calling out. This behavior is intended primarily to solicit praise for the ally rather than to protect a marginalized person.

When used responsibly, calling out is a powerful tool. It allows us to immediately interrupt bias and let the speaker know that their words or actions are unacceptable and will not be tolerated. Sometimes a hard stop is the only way to prevent further harm.

Calling in is a gentler, more inclusive way of registering bias. Calling in is preferable; however, which style is appropriate is situational and based on the severity of the maltreatment. I like to think of calling in as getting curious instead of furious. When I'm able to understand where that person is coming from and to establish a baseline of empathy, the "offender" is much more receptive to hearing how their comments or actions made me feel. If calling out is a hammer blow, calling in is a series of almost imperceptible fine-tunings.

It's quite common to feel anxious about calling a colleague in. Calling out is loud and active, and chances are, when a situation needs calling out, the harm is clear to all involved. You might get pushback from the person you're calling out, but probably not from the other witnesses.

Because calling in is private, it can feel a bit uncomfortable at the beginning. Most people don't like to be told they've done something hurtful, and it takes some vulnerability to explain to a colleague how you've been hurt. I've had a lot of opportunities to call in over the years and now make doing so a regular part of my communication with colleagues. I've found that making space for grace and understanding before engaging significantly increases the chances of a successful interaction.

Let me give you a real-life example.

I once attended a department retreat (which was just an extended department meeting in another building) where we talked about effective pedagogy and student engagement. One of my colleagues, a White female educator, complained that students of color weren't doing well in her classes. I asked what specific group of students were not doing well in her classes. I wanted to know more, so I asked whether the students were athletes, international students, Black, Latinx, or Asian students. I asked the question to get more information to help my colleague develop a plan that would hopefully allow her to better connect with the students and also to provide her with resources, such as clubs and study groups, that she could share with the specific group of students.

Her response was shocking and very telling. "BIPOC students just don't seem to get it," she said cavalierly.

Being an educator myself, and being a BIPOC, I called the person out right then and said the lack of empathy in her voice was undeniable and that if she admitted that BIPOC students weren't doing well in her class, but White students were, it was an indication that there might be some teacher bias going on. I encouraged her to review and revise her teaching techniques to ensure that *all* students learned and performed well.

Why did I call out rather than call in?

Well, first, being the only Black educator in the room, I felt it was my duty. Before I spoke up, I observed my other colleagues. Some of them put their heads down or looked away. They were also White and did not give any indication that they were going to address their White colleague's comments.

Second, I wanted everyone in the room to know that teacher bias is not okay. It is downright harmful and disgraceful. Empathy and equity must be present in the classroom. Empathy is a cornerstone of effective helping and is vital in understanding the experiences of others in a conscious or mindful way. I wanted those in attendance to shift their perspective.

What would you have done if you had observed that situation?

Let me offer you another example.

This is a story of Sam, a 24-year-old entrepreneur of color. Sam responded to a request for proposal for janitorial services that my former employer issued. Sam's company was one of three companies being interviewed for the contract. Sam's presentation was professional yet personable. Her passion for the work shone through. For those of you who asked yourselves, "How can anyone be passionate about janitorial work?", I need you to recognize and check your bias.

At the end of Sam's presentation, which was more potent than those of the other candidates, a few panelists asked questions. Sam asked panelists to repeat themselves and had a delayed response to some of the questions. Outwardly, it appeared that Sam was struggling. Sam revealed that she was experiencing hearing loss in her right ear and was trying to read lips. Panelists then spoke louder and slower so Sam could hear and better understand.

During the debrief, Tyler, the panelist with the longest tenure at the company, expressed his concern about Sam's age, race/ethnicity, disability, gender, and parental status. Nevertheless, the five-member panel voted unanimously to award the contract to Sam's janitorial company.

The next day, I invited Tyler out for coffee. (When you want to call someone in, invite them to one of the three C's: coffee, cupcakes, or cocktails.) During our outing, I asked Tyler to be specific about what it was about Sam's age, race/ethnicity, disability, gender, and parental status that led him to believe she was unqualified to receive the six-figure contract.

As I mentioned, Sam is a 24-year-old entrepreneur. She is an established business owner with great references. Sam's full name is Samantha; she identifies as female. I pointed out that, like many people, Sam chooses to go by a shortened name, just as Tyler preferred to be called Ty. Ty's argument that awarding Sam the contract could appear as racial tokenism did not hold water. The company touts supplier diversity, yet Ty was pushing back on those efforts. Ty then voiced his concern for Sam's hearing loss and her children. A person with implicit or unconscious bias would say, "I'm not against women working outside of the home, but I'm concerned that they might neglect their children." This is essentially what Ty was saying. I gently reminded him that, one, that was not our concern; and two, hearing loss does not impact a person's ability to clean and that Sam managed a crew that would do the job effectively and efficiently. I encouraged Ty to do what my Aunt Elnora has told me to do for years: "Think about what you're thinking about."

So, let me ask you: What would you have done if you had heard Tyler's comments? Would you have called him out, called him in, or said nothing? What would have prevented you from advocating for Sam?

Calling in starts with you and your frame of mind. Even though the person you are calling in has done something hurtful, that doesn't mean you have permission to return the attack. It's unkind, and more importantly, given the limits of time and emotional resources, being mean in return is ineffective.

It's quite likely that sometimes you'll be weary or frustrated when a call-in situation arises. These things are never convenient. Taking a minute to collect yourself and create psychological safety for yourself and for the person you're calling in significantly increases your chances of success. As you will know from your other relationships, when people feel respected and cared for, they have enough emotional bandwidth to be vulnerable, which means they can hear you when you explain how they've been hurtful without immediately becoming defensive and even doubling down. Vulnerability, mutual trust, and respect are the foundation of inclusive communication.

In a call-in situation, it is imperative that we put assumptions and our personal biases aside and ask questions that will help both parties get to a point of deeper understanding. Your role in a call-in is to inquire about the other person's point of view and to help them articulate it. As soon as your colleague senses a trap, they'll shut down and become defensive.

Here's an example of how to inquire and obtain more information during a call-in session:

What not to say: Why did you say X?
Ask this instead: What was your intention when you said X?

What not to say: Why do you think I'm wrong?

Ask this instead: How do you think another person might view this situation?

What not to say: Explain Y to me.

Ask this instead: Could you tell me more about Y?

Feedback is best given kindly, but clearly and constructively. Beating around the bush or minimizing the harm to make the person you're calling in feel better is counterproductive. It is possible to inflict real harm by accident, and that shouldn't be ignored. The goal of calling someone in is to help them evolve. Acknowledge that mistakes happen. Changing our behavior requires expanding our reference points and understanding different perspectives and experiences.

We've gone through this chapter with the assumption that you would be the person doing the calling in or out, that you are the more enlightened, progressive party doing the work to improve humanity. But sometimes you might make a mistake and find someone else is calling you out or in. Being publicly called out is emotionally difficult, both because it is embarrassing in the moment and then because later you have to reckon with the fact that you have caused actual harm to your colleagues. Being called in will probably also be embarrassing at first. With time, you'll see it as a constructive interaction. As you do the work to change your behavior, you'll probably be called in less often.

Your reaction to being called in or called out should be the same no matter what happens:

1. Think before you react. Even if the message is awkwardly delivered, the person calling you in or out is trying to make things better for individuals they believe have been mentally or emotionally injured.

2. Thank the person for sharing their feedback with you and ask any questions you have in the same open way you would if you were the one doing the calling in.

3. Apologize. If you publicly disparage and offend someone, you need to apologize publicly for having done so.

4. Engage in self-reflection. As Robert L. Rosen is often quoted as having said, "Self-reflection entails asking yourself questions about your values, assessing your strengths and failures, thinking about your perceptions and interactions with others, and imagining where you want to take your life in the future." Think about what the other person has said. What does it mean for your future behavior? What action will you take? Once you've decided on a course of action, carry it out—every day—until it becomes a habit.

Get ready for another Deep Dive. It contains a case study, discussion questions, and some questions for self-reflection. The chapter is designed, first, to help you be completely honest with yourself; second, to motivate the most creative part of you to find a solution; and third, to help you identify the ways you can be a genuine advocate.

Reflect

Do you believe it is divisive to call out systemic bias and institutional racism? Explain your answer.

5

DEEP DIVE

In this chapter, you'll find a case study and several questions for self-reflection and discussion.

If you're working through this book as a group, allow members adequate time to fully read and reflect individually, and then proceed with group discussion. Take the time to discuss things thoroughly and thoughtfully. You might not like what you hear initially, but giving your colleagues space to share is how we all grow.

Case Study

Jade Evans stood in front of the sink in the women's bathroom and tried to blink back her tears. She silently prayed that no one would barge in, notice her, and ask her if she was okay, as she simply was not in the mood to lie or engage in obligatory small talk. When Jade saw her reflection in the mirror, she realized that she was tired. It wasn't her body that was tired—it was her soul. Jade inhaled deeply.

What was she going to do? This job had started out as her dream job.

Last week Jade had graduated from a top-ranked university with her master's in industrial organizational psychology. Jade had received multiple job offers, but she chose to work at WHG. WHG was a technology company that created new health technologies and provided technician training. WHG was very close to Jade's home, which saved her time and money on commuting. The most alluring thing to Jade was that the hiring manager appreciated Jade's transparency and candidness during her interview when she expressed her desire to secure a position that would enable her to advance and be promoted once she'd completed her advanced degree. Fred Klein, the unit director, offered Jade the position of program coordinator in WHG's training department and offered to coach her. Fred agreed to sponsor and endorse Jade for promotion after she received her master's degree.

Jade loved and excelled at her job. However, being the only Black woman in the department, she often received warnings from other Black employees at WHG. One colleague said, "Don't be naïve about the promotion, and make sure you have an exit strategy. You're not the first and won't be the last." Jade discounted the warning and responded, "Oh, I'm sure I won't have any problems. Before I couldn't get promoted because I didn't have enough education. Now I'll have a master's, so there's nothing standing in my way. Fred assured me that I would be promoted. In fact, he coaches me." On this day, however, Jade realized that she should have paid more attention to what was being said.

The day started out fine, just like every other day. Jade spent the morning gathering information and preparing slides for her colleague Peter's upcoming technician training. Jade went to the break room to refill her water bottle and ran into Peter. She excitedly told him that she had finally completed her master's degree and would now apply for a promotion. She had been with WHG for three years; she felt that she'd proven herself and achieved a lot. She had a stellar track record. Peter was thrilled for Jade and said he looked forward to having her co-present with him soon rather than just perform administrative tasks.

Fred, Jade and Peter's director, quietly entered the room. He overheard the conversation and interrupted. In an agitated tone, Fred asked Jade, "Promotion? Promotion to what? Who do you think you are, Michelle Obama? The world only needs one of *her*."

Case Study Discussion Questions

1. If you were Jade, what would you have done in this moment?

2. If you were Peter, what would you have done in this moment?

3. What could Peter have done to advocate for Jade?

4. What should Jade do?

Self-Reflection

1. Describe a time when you were ignored, silenced, treated as less than, or given less than others. How did you feel? How often have you treated others the same way?

2. How can you shift your focus from a perception of race, gender, and personality to an ethic of character, competence, and contribution?

3. Do you believe it is divisive to call out systemic and institutional bias and racism? Explain your answer.

4. How can you advocate for marginalized colleagues?

6

ADVANCING FROM ADVOCATE
TO ACCOMPLICE

You might think it strange that I want you to become an accomplice. I get it. Accomplices commit crimes, right? Well, sort of. As all you *Law & Order* superfans know, accomplices are the ones supporting the action—the lookout, or the getaway car driver. It's the action part that I want you to lean into, as it is only through action that we will create a more equitable workplace and world.

Change doesn't happen in a vacuum. In addition to the hundreds of thousands of small steps we all take to advance the cause of quality, there need to be a few watershed moments—actions that move the needle significantly and irreversibly. If we look at any social movement, whether for civil rights, gay rights, or women's suffrage, we can see events like the Stonewall Riots, civil rights campaigning in the 1960s, or Ellen coming out on network television in 1997 as events that accelerated an already ongoing change. These kinds of changes can be violent, but they need not be. Engaging in civil disobedience, radically rejecting your privilege, and exposing your company to real losses because you're taking a stand are all equally valid accomplice actions.

The outcome for any accomplice action is to make the invisible visible, to acknowledge humanity and restore dignity.

Accomplices are the ones who are prepared to set their world on fire. They are the idealists who push the rest of us to be better. The difference between an advocate and an accomplice is the level of intensity and risk-taking. Accomplices will quit a job on principle or use their power to insist on terms of engagement that are fair to everyone.

Accomplices are on a mission, and any setback—social, financial or legal—is regarded as a temporary roadblock on their way to the larger goal.

Not everyone can be an accomplice. I think that's a good thing, for three reasons.

1. Some people have other responsibilities—they are the sole earner in their house, they are caring for dependants, or they are ill in some way or chronically underemployed. In those situations, the time, financial resources, or energy needed for big gestures are being used elsewhere.

2. The sort of needle-moving events that propel social change forward can't, by nature, take place all the time.

Resources are limited even for the most privileged, and after a while, accomplice actions become too familiar to be effective.

3. Big, splashy action only works in conjunction with the millions of smaller actions taken by advocates. It's like the way fire needs kindling to get started before it can burn the logs. Or the way a tsunami needs to absorb the energy of hundreds of smaller waves to become a threat. Without advocates, accomplices are just outliers.

In this section we'll look at three different ways to be an accomplice: Decry, Defy, and Dismantle.

As I've mentioned many times throughout this book, it is my opinion that some allies are virtue signalers who have an individualistic mindset and confuse invisibility with insignificance. Accomplices have a different outlook. They aren't afraid to get into "good trouble," as Representative John Lewis (1940–2020) advocated.

Accomplices understand that, as Sharon R. Hoover (2016) noted, "Any number of reasons can deliver the invisibility cloak: insecurity, loss, failure, injustice," and accomplices want to remove the veil and put the unseen on full view. Accomplices want not only to make the unseen visible, but also to acknowledge their humanity and restore their dignity. This can be accomplished only through action.

Accomplices experience and express outrage when their fellow human is mistreated; they educate themselves and encourage others to do the same; they take action and use whatever privileges they have to improve humanity. They are fine with taking risks and receiving negative publicity, because they are more concerned about the greater good than about temporary fallout. Accomplices decry, defy, and work to dismantle institutional discrimination.

Advocates leverage their privilege to help others rise. Accomplices renounce their privilege so that disadvantaged people can arrive themselves. It's the difference between giving someone a hand up over the wall and removing bricks so that no one else has to negotiate that barrier. Both are perfectly good solutions, but only one fixes the problem permanently.

Decry

Decrying—saying no—is essentially a bigger form of calling in and calling out. You can call it radical or aggressive. I like to think of it as unflinching. Many accomplices decry for a living. They are thought leaders, public intellectuals, and academics working in social justice, public policy, healthcare reform, prison reform, politics, and pretty much any other field you can think of. In general, they have the platform and the resources to make sure diversity, equity, and inclusion become part of the national discussion. The decrying may be professional, but that doesn't mean that it's easy or that it is supported by their employer. In all but a few places, accomplices are still at risk of losing their job if their boss decides they've had enough.

In December 2020, history professor Garrett Felber was fired from the University of Mississippi for calling out racist donors. Dr. Felber has researched and written about the Black freedom movement, mass incarceration, and immigrant detention. He received a $42,000 grant for a political education project titled "Study and Struggle." The dean allegedly rejected the grant in favor of a slightly larger one from a donor who does not support Dr. Felber's anti-racism activism.

In an interview with the *Mississippi Free Press* (as cited in Middleton, 2020), Dr. Felber said,

> It's been a challenge for me. I just continue to do the work. . . . Unfortunately, what it does, it makes that work much more difficult, and the weight is on faculty and largely those of us who, like in my own case, are untenured and have the most other responsibilities and the least protections.

Dr. Felber's termination has shined a light and opened discussion about departmental fundraising, donor dissatisfaction, academic freedom, and faculty autonomy and obligation. Non-tenured and tenure-track faculty are often considered invisible and insignificant. They go through a hell of a lot in order to receive the tarnished brass ring known as tenure.

With the recent hoopla surrounding Dr. Cornel West's departure from Princeton University after he was denied tenure and the recent denial of Nikole Hannah-Jones's tenure by the University of North Carolina Board of Trustees, there has been renewed (or maybe just louder) discussion about who is responsible for fixing the tenure system. Many place the onus on faculty. However, in a 2019 article published in *Diverse Issues in Higher Education*, Dr. Jeni Hart, professor of higher education and dean of the Graduate School at the University of Missouri, admitted that faculty who are minorities are structurally disadvantaged when it comes to getting tenure. She said that schools have to take responsibility for having plans and procedures that

> perpetuate racism, sexism, homophobia and all of those forms of discrimination . . . we should have a system where people can be successful without having to put a lot of emotional energy into figuring out how to navigate a system that wasn't meant for them. (para. 11)

Defy

If decrying is saying no, then defying is doing no—actively resisting instructions from bosses that further marginalize people, refusing to follow policies that harm others, actively not conforming to the privileged status quo.

In 1954, my favorite Golden Girl (and probably yours too), Ms. Betty White, was criticized for having a Black tap dancer, Arthur Duncan, on her self-titled show. Betty White told faultfinders, "I'm sorry. Live with it." She defied the critics and gave Arthur Duncan even more airtime. NBC canceled the show soon after (Fogerty, 2020). Betty White stood her ground against bigots. She was willing to lose her show, which she did, to hold on to her beliefs, which she did. Betty White is an accomplice.

Early in the morning on May 13, 2021, according to an article by Libby Brooks in *The Guardian*, Immigration Enforcement of Scotland showed up at a house in Pollokshields, a working-class neighborhood in Glasgow. It's something of a tough neighborhood, and community bonds are tight. The immigration officers rounded up asylum seekers from a house, but they were unable to move their van and transport the individuals to the deportation facility.

Why not?

Because a group of neighbors had surrounded the van to stop the deportation. More than 200 protesters gathered in the street in just a few hours and demanded that the immigration authorities let the people go.

"Let our neighbors go!" they chanted. One man lay under the van for eight hours to ensure the van could not drive away.

When the asylum seekers were finally released, protesters escorted them to the local mosque so they could celebrate Eid al-Fitr, one of the most important feast days in the Islamic year.

When I was an undergrad, I wanted to do a senior project on how Black male students are isolated and sometimes vilified. Since I was on the sports team, the athletic director was not okay with this. She accused me of gaslighting and of reverse discrimination. I told one of my former professors about it. She connected me with a professor at another university who was doing similar research. He invited me to assist him with the research, incorporated the research I had done for my senior project, and listed me as co-author on the paper. Not only was I able to achieve my research goal, but it also helped me get a scholarship to attend graduate school and become a public speaker. Both of the professors were my accomplices. —Michael M.

Scottish politicians fell over themselves making statements condemning the heavy-handedness of Immigration Enforcement. The Glasgow police also made it clear in statements that they had nothing to do with immigration enforcement and were only there to make sure the scene remained safe for everyone involved.

The protestors/protectors are accomplices.

Dismantle

Dismantling is the last step. By the time an idea is destroyed at the institutional level, people have been advocating and carrying out accomplice action for years—sometimes decades. When defying is the norm rather than an occasional action, institutions lose their power. It is then that laws, public policies, and the government can be reconfigured to reflect the new paradigm. Our current struggle for equality and equity is still in progress. There's still a long way to go.

Let me tell you a publicly known secret: I LOVE DOLLY PARTON! I sometimes get strange looks from people when I stay it out loud, but I do. I've been infatuated with Dolly Parton since I saw her and Kenny Rogers singing on the old TV show *Solid Gold* (damn, I'm getting old, but I still have a good memory!). I fell in love with Dolly even more when she expressed her support for Black Lives Matter. In an interview with *Billboard* in August 2020, Dolly said, "I understand people having to make themselves known and felt and seen. And of course Black lives matter. Do we think our little white asses are the only ones that matter? No!" I almost broke into a praise dance when she talked about changing the name of her business. She said, "When they said 'Dixie' was an offensive word, I thought, 'Well, I don't want to offend anybody.' ... As soon as you realize that something is a problem, you should fix it. Don't be a dumbass. That's where my heart is."

Why did this make me so happy? Because many people who claim to support social justice seem to backtrack and acquiesce when we need them to stand up and walk alongside us.

Actor Benedict Cumberbatch revealed that he'll only sign on for a role if he and his female co-stars receive the same salary (Jones, 2018). This right here is *huge*! A man, a White person, is willing to turn down a job. What?!! Fortunately, some are willing to make certain sacrifices. Alexis Ohanian, co-founder of Reddit, resigned from the company's board in summer 2020 and asked that he be replaced with a Black candidate (Hatmaker & Lundgren, 2020).

Celebrities aren't the only accomplices. Regular citizens are accomplices too.

In June 2020, according to Rahul Dubey as told to Justin Kirkland of *Esquire*, Dubey, who lived in Washington, DC, let 70 or so social justice protesters spend the night in his house to prevent them from being arrested for violating the city's curfew. According to news reports, Mr. Dubey and his neighbors sheltered and fed the strangers and helped the protestors clean the streets the next morning.

In December 2020, protesters in Portland, Oregon, chased off police who were trying to evict a family of color who had lived in the neighborhood for over 60 years.

Recently, the chief HR officer at one of my client organizations decided to demote herself and asked the board of directors to conduct a national search and give preference to candidates of color.

All of these people are accomplices. You can be one too.

I submitted a project proposal and was fortunate to be interviewed by the project lead. . . . I was scheduled to meet with the company's CEO and executive team. The project lead called me and gave me additional information that she thought would be helpful for me to include in my upcoming presentation. She said the executive team often overlooked boutique firms like mine because they didn't think smaller companies had the capacity and capability to scale these types of projects. She thought it was unfair. Providing information was her way of creating equity. I was selected as the consultant of choice because the project lead served as my accomplice, not just my advocate. —Isabella H.

Get ready for the final Deep Dive. As usual, it contains a case study, discussion questions, and some questions for self-reflection. Be completely honest with yourself, tap into the most creative parts of yourself to find a solution, and identify the ways you can become an accomplice.

Reflect

What does radical activism look like to you?
Why does it look that way?

7

DEEP DIVE

In this chapter, you'll find a case study and several questions for self-reflection and discussion.

If you're working through this book as a group, allow members adequate time to fully read and reflect individually, then proceed with group discussion. Take the time to thoroughly and thoughtfully discuss things. You might not like what you hear initially, but giving your colleagues space to share is how we all grow.

Case Study

"You have a collect call from Tiana from the Wyoming Women's Center. Do you accept the call?" the operator asked.

"What? Yes, yes, I'll accept."

"Mark?" Tiana whimpered. Her face was flushed and her hands trembled as she held the phone up to her ear. She was trying to stave off a panic attack.

"Tiana, I've been so worried about you. What's going on?" Mark asked.

"Look, Mark, I'm going to be honest with you. You know I took vacation time to visit my family in Denver. Well, Jason and I decided to drive down. We got pulled over in Wyoming and arrested for having marijuana and an open container of alcohol. We weren't drinking and driving, but we got arrested for having it," Tiana explained.

"Oh my god!" Mark responded.

Tiana continued, "I honestly didn't think it was a big deal. I pled guilty and the judge sentenced me to 90 days in prison." Tiana broke down crying. "I'm calling to let you know and to give you my resignation."

"What? Resignation? I'm not letting you resign," Mark countered.

"I'm in prison on a drug charge, and The Lifeless Company has strict employment rules," Christina said.

"You are a top performer, not only in Seattle, but also regionally," Mark answered. "Many of us, myself included, have been in a rough spot at some point. Don't worry about it—I got you. As far as I'm concerned, you're simply on leave. Got it? Call me when you need to. I'll see you when you get back."

The next day, Mark sent an all-staff email stating that Tiana was on an emergency leave of absence and temporarily reassigning her job duties. That same day, Mark did some investigating, found the judge who had handled Tiana's case, and sent an email on Tiana's behalf. Mark explained that although he understood and respected that recreational and medicinal marijuana use was illegal in Wyoming (at least at that time), it was legal in Washington State and in Colorado, which is where Tiana and her fiancé were heading at the time of their arrest. Mark noted that he had known Tiana for years; that she was not a "typical chronic marijuana user"; and that she was, instead, a highly effective, efficient, top-producing team member whom he had groomed to succeed him as director. Mark also revealed that earlier in his life, he had struggled with drug and alcohol addiction. He had been arrested several times and firmly believed he received grace and mercy not only from the judicial system, but also from the corporate system because of White male privilege. Mark provided statistics and data about institutional and societal barriers faced by Black women in the United States, including federal policies and regulations and workforce studies. Mark noted that he was neither as brilliant nor as resilient as Tiana and that it was his hope that grace and mercy would be extended to Tiana as well. Mark pleaded for Tiana's early release and for her record to be expunged so she could have not only a successful career, but also a fruitful life.

Case Study Discussion Questions

1. If you were Tiana, would you have informed Mark of your situation?

2. Do you agree with Mark's decision to put Tiana on a leave of absence, or do you think he should have terminated her? Explain your answer.

3. How do you feel about Mark's decision to contact the judge in Tiana's case?

4. How else could Mark have shown Tiana support without contacting the judge or placing Tiana on a leave of absence?

Self-Reflection

1. What privileges do you have in society? Who granted you these privileges? Why don't others have these same privileges?

2. How often do you make space for others without being asked to?

3. Think of a time when you sacrificed your "piece of the pie" for a marginalized colleague or friend. What were the benefits and consequences of your actions?

4. Think of a time when you stood up for a person of color or someone from a marginalized group. What was the person's response to your attempt to help?

8

FINAL THOUGHTS

I thank you and congratulate you for taking this bold step to learn how to move from a performative ally to a genuine advocate for marginalized people. I hope you will be courageous enough to become an accomplice. Moving from an ally to an accomplice is not a glam gig; it is intentional, sometimes intense, lifelong work.

An ally approves of (or simply does not complain about) anti-racist work and DEI efforts, but is not willing to actively engage or support the efforts in a meaningful way. They have an individualistic mindset and seldom consider the collective. Allies temporarily stand beside marginalized people and offer limited support. They may listen, but they will not walk with those who have been stigmatized, discriminated against, or treated unfairly through their experience. Allies proclaim that they are "good," but that implies that someone else is not. They tend to be fragile when you remind them of the light and shadow of their perceived goodness and to engage in cognitive, emotional, and/or behavioral avoidance rather than having a fruitful, life-altering conversation.

An advocate, from my perspective, is a person from an empowered group who acts to help an oppressed group. Advocates support and promotes anti-racist work and DEI efforts. They walk beside, and sometimes in front of, a marginalized person to hold the open the door for them. Advocates sympathize and show compassion. They listen and educate themselves but sometimes engage in behavioral avoidance (i.e., feeling helpless or hopeless). They understand that emotions are temporary, and they don't allow emotions to stop them from advocating for and supporting social justice movements.

An accomplice is a person from an empowered group who uses their privilege to stand up and speak out for a person or group that is targeted and discriminated against. Accomplices actively engage in anti-racist work and DEI efforts. An accomplice works to end oppression by going to bat for people who are stigmatized, discriminated against, or treated unfairly and actively tries to protect them from harm. In other words, accomplices don't sit idly by; they are willing to act with and for oppressed peoples and accept the potential fallout for doing so, even if it costs them the benefits of their power. Accomplices understand the risk it takes to see the change they believe is necessary and work to dismantle the power structure of White privilege and supremacy and create substantial and sustainable societal and institutional change that means all persons are treated with dignity and respect. They walk beside, in front of, and behind marginalized people while recognizing and respecting the fact that the marginalized individual or group is the expert and knows what is best for them.

I hope you all accept the Allyship Challenge. To move from an ally to an accomplice, do the following:

Step 1 – Reflect on Your Privilege

Step 2 – Educate Yourself

Step 3 – Develop and Expand Your Cross-Cultural Relationships

Step 4 – Communicate

Step 5 – Practice Compassionate Listening

Step 6 – Understand Your Discomfort

Step 7 – Consider Other Perspectives

Step 8 – Engage

Step 9 – Call In or Call Out

Step 10 – Amplify Marginalized Voices

Step 11 – Defy, Decry, and Dismantle

Step 12 – Practice and Encourage L.E.A.D.

Step 1 – Reflect on Your Privilege

"Privilege" is a term that makes some people bristle. The idea of "White privilege" took hold in 1988 when scholar Peggy McIntosh published her seminal work, *White Privilege: Unpacking the Invisible Knapsack*. Although Dr. McIntosh's article focuses primarily on race, privilege also relates to gender, sexuality, age, ability status, and, of course, class. Privilege is an unearned advantage that allows a person to enjoy special rights with impunity. Diversity and White privilege consultant Dr. Francis Kendall defined privilege in 2002 as "having greater access to power and resources than people of color [in the same situation] do" (p. 1). Privilege exists because of historic inequities and continues to influence systemic decisions. Let's be clear: We all have a specific privilege. Once you understand your privilege, what can you do challenge the status quo?

Step 2 – Educate Yourself

Educate yourself and encourage others to do the same. It is acceptable to ask questions on occasion, but you have the power and the responsibility to educate yourself without interrogating your colleagues. Instead of burdening individuals from marginalized groups with rapid-fire questions, check in with Google or Siri. If necessary, you can approach your friends or colleagues for clarification about things you may not fully understand. Reading books is great, but what good is knowledge if you don't engage in conversation and share what you've learned? Talk about what you've learned and encourage others to expand their knowledge base by sharing articles, books, films, and other resources.

Step 3 – Develop and Expand Your Cross-Cultural Relationships

In cross-cultural relationships, it's common to defend your own culture and to make assumptions about your partner's culture. Cultural stereotypes are a source of misunderstanding and often kill a discussion before it even starts. Instead of relying on stereotypes, focus on personality, beliefs, and opinions. Find out why a different cultural group has certain habits, beliefs, and traditions before comparing it with your own culture. And try to look at their way of living through their eyes. Remember, though: It is not enough for us to acknowledge differences in others; we need to acknowledge the oppression they experience as well.

Step 4 – Communicate

We all have had experiences that have shaped who we are and how we think about certain things, people, and situations. We need to be brave enough to share our perspectives and how we came to our conclusions and to ask and encourage others to do the same. Communication provides us with an opportunity to experience a moral, intellectual, and social shift. However, we should not try to impose our will or our mindset on others. We can and should encourage others to be open-minded and to consider our perspectives and feelings; but demanding that they do so will not have the result we want. We must expect and accept nonclosure and continue to learn and grow through relationships and shared experiences.

Step 5 – Practice Compassionate Listening

Listening requires your ears, your eyes, and your heart. Compassionate listening encourages people to express themselves honestly and fully. Compassionate listening is non-judgmental and non-adversarial. The listener "strives to see through any masks of hostility and fear to the sacredness of the individual" (Cohen, 2011, p. 10).

To become a compassionate listener, an individual must develop empathy, suspend judgment, respect others, and communicate with an open heart. Empathy is the ability to understand another person's feelings. When you practice empathy, you connect with another person and develop a deeper understanding of their behavior, motivations, and life experience. Try to put yourself in the speaker's shoes and identify with their experience. Amazing conversations are born when you overcome your biases, put your presumptions on the back burner, let go of expectations, and fully listen to the speaker's perspective with an open mind. Instead of trying to dominate the conversation, show respect by asking thoughtful, open-ended questions in an attempt to understand the speaker's opinions and perspectives. Listen closely and avoid interrupting. An open heart enables you listen and speak in a caring, curious, fair, and supportive way.

Step 6 – Understand Your Discomfort

Many people find having courageous conversations about bias and xenophobia difficult or uncomfortable. We prefer to avoid conflict. We evade conversations, and as a result, we are denying people's lived realities.

Failing to address the elephant in the room and have courageous conversations does a disservice to all the parties involved, on both a personal and a professional level. According to Columbia University Professor Derald Wing Sue, avoidance comes in three forms: cognitive avoidance, emotional avoidance, and behavioral avoidance. Each form causes harm and pain. As Sue (2015) noted, "These avoidance strategies actually make them [people] appear *more* biased and prejudiced" (p. 14).

To understand your discomfort, you must first be vulnerable enough to acknowledge your fears. Are you afraid that you will stumble over your words or be inarticulate? Is your discomfort the result of not being aware of history or current events? Acknowledge your emotions. Use a 6-point Likert scale to assess your discomfort level. Are you *completely uncomfortable, very uncomfortable, somewhat uncomfortable, somewhat comfortable, very comfortable,* or *completely comfortable*?

Work through the discomfort. The more you practice facilitating courageous conversations in a safe space, the better you will manage discomfort. Consider the benefits of effectively resolving a conflict through courageous conversations and the consequences you may experience if you fail to do so.

Step 7 – Consider Other Perspectives

"Reality" is defined by society, and as humans living in a specific society, our perceptions of reality are based on shared assumptions. People in a specific society accept an understanding as reality; it "becomes policy, [and] ideas about power and privilege in the community become codified" (Vinney, 2019, para. 10). Social constructs are not fixed; knowledge is often altered based on historical, political, and economic conditions.

Because of our culture and upbringing, we all bring a unique social construction of knowledge to the table. As Trenholm and Jensen (2013) noted, "The way we perceive the world affects the way we live in it" (p. 131). We must consider the origins of our and others' "knowledge" and realize that it is inherited, interpreted, and modified by each generation.

Step 8 – Engage

Staying engaged and being objective will enable you not only to communicate, but also to truly connect with others. Try to understand the other person's perspective; anticipate possible reactions and consider how to keep the conversation moving in a positive way. Do not turn the interaction into a personal attack or assume that it is one.

Step 9 – Call In or Call Out

Many people wrestle with the decision to "call out" versus "call in." "Calling out" allows us to immediately interrupt bias; it is a hard stop intended to prevent further harm. Calling out lets the speaker know that their words or actions are unacceptable and will not be tolerated. "Calling in" is a gentler, more inclusive way of registering bias. Calling in is preferable; however, which style is appropriate is situational and based on the severity of the maltreatment.

Calling out is appropriate to halt microinsults and microattacks. "Calling in" is an appropriate action when there is no imminent threat or harm. For example, when a person's implicit bias is showing, it is fitting to call them in and make them aware of it and encourage them to resolve their hidden prejudice. Calling in means we are seeking to learn more about someone's perspective, to gain a mutual sense of understanding.

Step 10 – Amplify Marginalized Voices

Rather than hijacking an idea, give credit to colleagues for their thoughts, and offer to collaborate with them rather than compete with them. Read works by people of color and other marginalized people; help them share their message.

Step 11 – Defy, Decry, and Dismantle

Say no, actively resist, and work to tear down and rebuild the entire system and institutional structure.

Step 12 – Practice and Encourage L.E.A.D.

It is our privilege and our responsibility as humans, communicators, and colleagues to create an atmosphere of Love, Enthusiasm, Awareness, and Development.

In *All About Love*, hooks (2000) stated, "To truly love we must learn to mix various ingredients—care, affection, recognition, respect, commitment, and trust, as well as honest and open communication" (p. 5).

In line with this definition is a quote from James Baldwin (1989, p. 156), who said, "If I love you, I have to make you conscious of the things you don't see."

Enthusiasm can yield outstanding results in the area of communication. By showing enthusiasm and commitment to justice, we are letting all those concerned know that we genuinely want to learn and grow and experience a moral, intellectual, social, and/or emotional shift.

Awareness means being self-aware of your privilege, discomfort, ego, and values, thoughtfully demonstrating those values to others, and inspiring others to do the same. Awareness is the key component of emotional intelligence. It is crucial that we self-regulate our emotions while also tuning in to others' feelings and their fear or concern about judgment and/or retribution.

Development is a continuous process of improvement. Personal development starts from within. A person who clearly cares about development routinely engages in reflective practice and is ready and willing to listen to and encourage others along the way. Development will help us to speak our truth with confidence and kindness in a respectful manner, meaning we will become a compassionate listener rather than reactive. It is only through L.E.A.D. that we all get free.

In closing, I encourage you all to use your privilege for good and to move from ally to accomplice. Remember what ally stands for:

A: Admit you aren't knowledgeable about certain things and don't know what to say or do.

L: Listen to different perspectives.

L: Lean into your discomfort and examine why you are uncomfortable.

Y: Yield to the experience of the person being harmed instead of gaslighting the individual.

Move toward being an accomplice. Encourage others to acknowledge, share, and confront their fears rather than demonstrate hostility and argumentativeness.

Be an accomplice. Stand up and speak up for those who cannot speak for themselves; rally around those who are wrongfully attacked.

Be an accomplice. Help heal the wounded spirit.

Reflect

How do you show love to your immediate community? How can you expand or replicate that love outside of your community?

In the mission statement for Project Semicolon, Amy Bleuel said, "Stay strong; love endlessly; change lives." What does this mean to you?

How will you invite others to join you on this journey of moving from a virtue-signaling performative ally to an action-taking, privilege-sharing accomplice?

REFERENCES

Andreoni, J. (1989). Giving with impure altruism: Applications to charities and Ricardian equivalence. *Journal of Political Economy, 97*(6), 1447–1458. https://doi.org/10.1086/261662

Andrews-Dyer, H. (2015, June 23). Actress Meryl Streep sends a letter to each and every member of Congress. The Washington Post. https://www.washingtonpost.com/news/reliable-source/wp/2015/06/23/actress-meryl-streep-sends-a-letter-to-each-and-every-member-of-congress/

Baldwin, J. (1989). *Conversations with James Baldwin.* F. R. Standley & D. D. Pratt, Eds. University Press of Mississippi.

Ben & Jerry's. Issues we care about. https://www.benjerry.com/values/issues-we-care-about

Bluel, A. Brooks, L. (2021, May 14). 'A special day': How a Glasgow community halted immigration raid. *The Guardian.* https://www.theguardian.com/uknews/2021/may/14/a-special-day-how-glasgow-community-halted-immigration-raid

Chugh, D. (n.d.). *The myth of the good person* [Interview]. Goop. https://goop.com/wellness/mindfulness/the-myth-of-the-good-person/

Chugh, D. (2018). *The person you mean to be: How good people fight bias*. HarperCollins.

Cohen, A. S. (2011). *Practicing the art of compassionate listening*. The Compassionate Listening Project.

Davies, H. J. (2019, March 16). Culture's race problem: 'For white hipsters, blackness is a thing to consume but not engage with.' *Guardian*. https://www.theguardian.com/culture/2019/mar/16/cultures-race-problem-for-white-hipsters-blackness-is-a-thing-to-consume-but-not-engage-with

Desta, Y. (2018, January 25). Watch Octavia Spencer explain how Jessica Chastain helped her make five times her salary. *Vanity Fair*. https://www.vanityfair.com/hollywood/2018/01/octavia-spencer-jessica-chastain-salary

Downey, S. N., van der Werff, L., Thomas, K. M., & Plaut, V. C. (2015). The role of diversity practices and inclusion in promoting trust and employee engagement. *Journal of Applied Social Psychology, 45*(1), 35–44. http://doras.dcu.ie/22239/1/Diversity_and_Engagement-_Final_Accepted_Submission.pdf

Ferguson, J. T. (2016). About. https://www.tietheknot.org/about

Fogerty, P. (2020, October 8). *Arthur Duncan on the Betty White shows why Betty White is "the first lady of television."*

HITC. https://www.hitc.com/en-gb/2020/10/08/the-betty-white-show-arthur-duncan-cancelled/

Fukuyama, F. (1997). Social capital and the modern capitalist economy: Creating a high trust workplace. *Stern Business Magazine, 4*(1). https://www.socialcapitalresearch.com/trust-and-trustworthiness/

Gardenswartz, L., Cherbosque, J., & Rowe, A. (2008). *Emotional intelligence for managing results in a diverse world.* Black.

Goleman, D. (1995). *Emotional intelligence.* Bantam Books.

Gray, J. M. (2018, October 1). *Performing wokeness.* Harvard Crimson. https://www.thecrimson.com/column /better-left-unsaid/article/2018/10/1/gray-performing-wokeness/

Guerilus, S. (2020, December 9). *Portland protestors chase off police trying to evict Black family.* Grio. https://thegrio.com /2020/12/09/portland-protestors-chase-off-police-evict-black-family/

Hatmaker, T., & Lundgren, I. (2020, June 5). Alexis Ohanian steps down from Reddit board, asks for his seat to go to a black board member. https://techcrunch.com/2020/06/05/alexis-ohanian-steps-down-reddit-board/

Hollis, L. P. (2012). *Bully in the ivory tower: How aggression and incivility erode American higher education.* Patricia Berkley.

hooks, bell. (2000). *All about love: New visions.* Harper.

Hoover, S. (2016). *Insignificant until finding the One Who Sees Me.* http://sharonrhoover.com/2016/06/13 /insignificant/

Jones, P. (2018, May 13). Benedict Cumberbatch: I'll turn down a role if my female co-star isn't paid the same. RadioTimes.com. https://www.radiotimes.com/tv/drama/benedict-cumberbatch-equal-pay-women-female-co-star-patrick-melrose/

Kendall, F. E. (2002). *Understanding White privilege: Creating pathways to authentic relationships across race.* Routledge.

Kettler, S. (2019, January 30; updated 2020, September 15). *Ella Fitzgerald and Marilyn Monroe: Inside their surprising friendship.* Biography. https://www.biography.com/news/marilyn-monroe-ella-fitzgerald-friendship

Kirkland, J. (2020, June 2). A 2 a.m. talk with Rahul Dubey, the 'absolute legend' sheltering Black Lives Matter protesters. *Esquire.* https://www.esquire.com/news-politics/a32742452/rahul-dubey-dc-black-lives-matter-protesters-shelter/

Marquis, C. (2020, June 9). *Why Ben & Jerry's won't stay silent on white supremacy—Or other social justice issues.* Forbes.com. https://www.forbes.com/sites/christophermarquis/2020/06/09/why-ben--jerrys-wont-stay-silent-on-white-supremacy-or-other-social-justice-issues/?sh=35f54f646f07

Mayer, R. C., Davis, J. H., & Schoorman, F. D. (1995). An integrative model of organizational trust. *Academy of Management Review, 20*(3), 709–734. https://doi.org/10.2307/258792

McGregor, D. (1960). *The human side of enterprise.* McGraw-Hill.

McIntosh, P. (1988). *White privilege: Unpacking the invisible knapsack.* Women's International League for Peace and Freedom.

Middleton, C. (2020, December 15). UM fires history professor who criticizes 'powerful, racist donors' and 'carceral state.' *Mississippi Free Press.* https://www.mississippifreepress.org/7518/um-fires-history-professor-who-criticizes-powerful-racist-donors-and-carceral-state/

Nhat Hanh, T. (2010, March). Oprah talks to Thich Nhat Hanh [Interview]. Oprah.com. https://www.oprah.com/spirit/oprah-talks-to-thich-nhat-hanh

Newman, M. (2020, August 15). *Dolly Parton steers her empire through the pandemic—and keeps it growing.* Billboard. https://www.billboard.com/articles/columns/country/9432581/dolly-parton-country-power-players-billboard-cover-story-interview-2020

Nichols, C. (n.d.). *The good guy/bad guy myth.* Aeon. https://aeon.co/essays/why-is-pop-culture-obsessed-with-battles-between-good-and-evil

Nichols, R. G., & Stevens, L. A. (1957). Listening to people. *Harvard Business Review.* https://hbr.org/1957/09/listening-to-people

Owens, E. (2017, August 14). *OPINION: White people, only you can stop the next Charlottesville.* City Life. https://www.phillymag.com/news/2017/08/14/charlottesville-white-responsibility/

Patrick, B. C., Hisley, J., Kempler, T., & College, G. (2000). "What's everybody so excited about?": The effects of teacher enthusiasm on student intrinsic motivation and vitality. https://doi.org/10.1080/00220970009600093

Peck, M. Scott. (1992). *The road less traveled: A new psychology of love, traditional values and spiritual growth.* Career Track.

Phillips, L. T., & Lowery, B. S. (2015). The hard-knock life? Whites claim hardships in response to racial inequity. *Journal of Experimental Social Psychology, 61*, 12-18. https://doi.org/10.1016/j.jesp.2015.06.008

Stewart, P. (2019, October 30). *Scholars decry discrimination in tenure review process*. Diverse Issues in Higher Education. https://diverseeducation.com/article/158582/

Sue, D. W. (2015). *Race talk and the conspiracy of silence*. Wiley.

Trenholm, S., & Jensen, A. (2013). *Interpersonal communication* (7th ed.). Oxford University Press.

Uwagba, O. (2020). *Whites: On race and other falsehoods*. HarperCollins.

Vinney, C. (2019, March 28). *Social constructionism definition and examples*. ThoughtCo. https://www.thoughtco.com /social-constructionism-4586374

Walker, A. (1983). *In search of our mother's gardens: Womanist prose*. Harcourt Brace Jovanovich.

Williams, D. (2020, June 3). *This man sheltered dozens of protesters in his Washington, DC, home to protect them from arrest*. CNN. https://www.cnn.com/2020/06/02/us /dc-protesters-sheltered-trnd/index.html

ABOUT THE AUTHOR

Dr. Kimberly Harden is a diversity strategist, an award-winning educator, and a keynote speaker. As founder and CEO of Harden Consulting Group, LLC, Kimberly helps organizations shift from a traditional diversity and inclusion model to a model that emphasizes equity and belonging.

Kimberly serves as a professor in the Department of Communication at Seattle University. Before she became an educator, she spent over 15 years working in the healthcare sector. Kimberly is passionate about justice, leadership, care, and transformation. She has spoken at numerous conferences, including the International Leadership Association Conference, the Be on the Rise Diversity and Inclusion Summit, Ignite Seattle's Education Lab, and the One Woman Fearless! Summit.

Kimberly received her undergraduate degree in Communication from The University of Washington, a master's degree in Communication and Leadership Studies from Gonzaga University, and a doctorate in Educational Leadership from Concordia University. She wholeheartedly agrees with Aristotle's assertion that "educating the mind without educating the heart is no education at all."

For more information, visit www.hardenconsultinggroup.com.

Made in the USA
Middletown, DE
19 March 2023

26965286R00076